BRANDING

for

TIPS TO GROW YOUR
ONLINE AUDIENCE &
MAXIMIZE YOUR INCOME

BLOGGERS

ZACH HELLER

ALLWORTH PRESS
NEW YORK

Special Thanks to:

Emily Rapp
http://ourlittleseal.wordpress.com
Little Seal

Zac Johnson
http://zacjohnson.com
zacjohnson.com

Robin Callan
http://roomfu.com/blog
Fu For Thought

Pamela Wilson
http://www.bigbrandsystem.com
Big Brand Systems

Rosalind Gardner
http://rosalindgardner.com
Rosalind Gardner

Andrew Boer & Andrew Eisner
http://www.movablemedia.com
Movable Media

Liz Strauss
http://www.successful-blog.com
Successful-Blog

Michela Chiucini
webislove.com
Web is Love

Jay Johnson
http://www.design2share.com
Design2Share

Published by Allworth Press
An imprint of Skyhorse Publishing, Inc.
307 West 36th Street, 11th Floor
New York, NY 10018
www.skyhorsepublishing.com and www.allworth.com

Allworth Press books may be purchased in bulk at special discounts for sales promotion, corporate gifts, fund-raising, or educational purposes. Special editions can also be created to specifications. For details, contact the Special Sales Department, Allworth Press, 307 West 36th Street, 11th Floor, New York, NY 10018 or info@skyhorsepublishing.com.

Copublished by New York Institute of Career Development.
New York Institute of Career Development is a registered trademark of Distance Education Co. LLC in the United States and/or other countries
211 East 43rd Street, Suite 2402
New York, NY 10017
www.nyicd.com, blog.nyicd.com, and www.decnyc.com

Cover and Interior Page Design by Keith Gallagher
Editorial Writing by Zach Heller
Editing by Steven Evans
Preface by Andrew Boer
NYICD Publisher: Jay Johnson
NYICD Director: Chuck DeLaney

Library of Congress Cataloging-in-Publication Data has been applied for and is on file with the Publisher.

ISBN: 978-1-62153-248-4
Printed in China.

CONTENTS

PREFACE

The Valuation of Content
By Andrew Boer
President, Movable Media

Spend some time on any New England beach and some well-meaning soul may point out that the beautiful purple-tinged Quahog clam shells strewn across the sands were once used as currency by Native Americans. But even a child can quickly appreciate why wampum beads were not destined for greatness: they're a plentiful resource that once required intensive labor to convert into beads. But with modern tools, they'd require relatively little effort to manufacture and duplicate.

In our modern content economy, words have become wampum. Words, generally speaking, are increasingly cheap to produce and available in a seemingly infinite supply. Words are now manufactured into content on a massive scale by both humans and computers alike. Content has become so devalued that the most successful publishers in the past decade have been those whose business models revolve around paying nearly nothing for content.

The resulting explosion of cheap, mediocre content has meant that as readers, we've become awash in noise.

And many content creators are now as nervous as a 17th century clamdigger. We think at least part of the problem is how content is currently valued: a word count makes a lousy predictor of value.

Like wampum, a word count is a kind of proxy for the cost of creation, the time and craft of the creator. In the print journalism world, a cost-based approach to content made sense. An article of 500 words might be a perfectly acceptable predictor of value if the article filled a certain amount of physical space in a publication that was accompanied by paid ad pages or subscription revenue. Individually, the article might have very little measurable effect on the overall revenue of the publication.

Online content, however, is a different beast. It tends to stand alone and generate revenue independently of the rest of the content.

When it comes to revenue (value), one 500-word article is simply not like another.

Of course, publishers and authors aren't truly pricing "by the word." They try to use other proxies to determine a fair price, including the subject matter, the "market rate," and the reputation, experience, and expertise of the author. But these intangibles also make poor containers of value, in the sense that they're also not helpful in predicting whether an article will find an audience.

If a publisher can't predict the revenue a 500-word article will create based on quality or reputation, they eventually turn to price to choose a content provider. As cheaper alternatives enter the market, prices for content rapidly start to decline.

All of this has been happening in the publishing world for the past ten years, and it's painted a fairly grim picture for bloggers and other content creators and publishers alike: lower wages and more noise.

But in the past couple years, a new and predictable way to value content has emerged that's transforming the content economy. Many bloggers have begun to develop a built-in following through social networks and search engines, which are becoming a legitimate new channel for content distribution. We call this "the Author Channel."

THE AUTHOR CHANNEL

With the advent of social media and author ranked search, authors (that's *you*, if you're a blogger) now have a surprising amount of control, in aggregate, over content distribution. On sites like *Forbes.com*, over 50% of the traffic now comes from the audiences of its own contributors.

Authors now have the ability to build audiences on their own blogs and move them, which allows them to predictably affect the value of their content. Soon they'll be compensated according to tangible yardsticks of value such as audiences and engagement, and per-word pricing will disappear.

The beauty of this new author channel is that it realigns the value created by authors and bloggers with the value captured by publishers and brands.

They're now both speaking the same language.

This may also help solve the "noise" problem, as the audiences of successful creators grow in direct proportion to the authors' quality and expertise. Indeed, the search engines are beginning to focus on signals like "Author Rank" and "engagement" instead of "Page Rank" to determine the primacy of content.

Soon publishers will work with bloggers to develop market rates not for the words of the content they create, but for the attention of the audience they hope to bring. While this model of performance-based "entrepreneurial journalism" was pioneered at the low end by search-based "content farms" like Demand Media, incentive-based compensation actually turns out to be most effective for premium content creators such as Seeking Alpha, *Huffington Post,* and Forbes, where authors have significant social followings.

Of course when freelance journalists, bloggers, and influencers of all stripes are compensated based on audience distribution and not an arbitrary "per-word" rate, they'll become essentially indistinguishable from publishers of custom content.

SO CONTENT IS NOT ENOUGH: BUILD YOUR AUDIENCE

For authors, this approach means that they'll soon be expected to manage (and be compensated for) many of the distribution responsibilities that have been the purview of publishers. Having a large social distribution network and search presence in this new world takes on substantially enhanced importance.

The good news is those bloggers who can deliver an audience by engaging the public with their distinctive brands will be able to capture much more value from a content transaction. Content has become a commodity, but the attention of a target audience is inherently limited, and can never be commoditized.

The future of media, then, is a single transparent currency shared across the digital ecosystem between authors, brands, and publishers, through which value is measured and exchanged.

And that currency is audience, not words.

Understanding how to maximize the valuation of the currency is critical to maximizing your value as a blogger.

INTRODUCTION

You are a brand.
Sorry to blow your mind like that right off the bat, but it's true.

Whether you want to be or not, whether intended or by accident, you already are one. There is something, or some things, that define you. It's how people know you, what they expect from you, and what they think of you. It's an extension of your personality.

Think back on your high school days. They may be long past or they may be very recent. Perhaps they're long past but feel like they were just yesterday. Can't remember them? Then think of any classic high school drama on TV or the big screen.

High school is the perfect metaphor for understanding what I mean when I talk about your brand. In high school, branding is simple. Brands form due to the separation of and assimilation into distinct groups of people that are defined by what others think of them.

You have the jocks, the cheerleaders, the band geeks, the nerds, the Goths, the punks, the partiers, the popular kids, the smart kids, etc. Regardless of whether or not your high school was as cliché as the ones usually featured in the movies, you know who each of these groups are. You can form a picture in your head of the individuals represented in each one. You know how you expect them to act, talk, and interact with each other and with members of the other groups. You know how teachers and other authority figures treat them.

And while all of our preconceived notions about who these people are may be dead wrong, it doesn't change the fact that we think these things. These groups each have a brand.

WHAT IS A BRAND?

Wikipedia defines a brand as a "name, term, design, symbol, or any other feature that identifies one seller's good or service as distinct from those of other sellers." For large corporations, a brand usually includes everything from the logo of the company, to the way they speak and sell to consumers, to the way they treat their employees and customers and the way they service their products.

A strong brand comes to define a company and everything that they do. The brand guides their actions, and those actions in turn help to support the brand. It's part culture, part identity.

Most people lump a definition of the term "brand" together with "branding."

While I feel that the two are related, it's important to identify the difference. Marketing consultant Kristin Zhivago articulates the distinction quite well:

"Branding is the promises you make. Your brand is the promises you keep."

Your brand is the way customers (or readers) experience your product (or blog). Branding is the art of creating, defining, and controlling that brand. Companies undertake branding and rebranding efforts in order to try to solidify or restore their image in the minds of consumers.

MAC VERSUS PC

Apple is a great company to refer to when talking about branding. They know who they are, and they spend millions of dollars every year reinforcing that image. Think back on the series of commercials that ran from 2006 to 2009. They were referred to as the Mac/PC ads, and they featured John Hodgman as the "corporate," uptight PC, and Justin Long is the "hip," smooth Mac.

In 2010, *Adweek* declared this series of ads to be the best advertising campaign of the first decade of the new century. The goal of these commercials, which were some of the most successful in the company's long history of powerful television ads, was to reinforce the brand as it was seen by most Apple customers. Macs ran better than PCs, but more than that, they were just cooler.

Apple has done a great job of becoming, and remaining, "cool." Mac users, and Apple fans in general, believe that they are choosing the best products. And while they may be, this strong sense of hipness that comes with being an Apple user is playing a strong role in their decision process, even if it's so far under the surface that they can't admit to it.

The Mac/PC commercials drove this idea home. By portraying "Mac" as a young, casually dressed, witty counterpart to PC's traditional, corporate, dull style, the look of the ads did just as much for the brand as the actual dialogue. This is branding.

John Hodgman as PC and Justin Long as Mac in Apple's Get a Mac Ad Campaign.

WHEN GOOD BRANDS GO BAD

Brands come to define a company. Most times the way people view a company is part of the master plan. It's a positive association that customers of the company have, and can be used to attract new customers. It was planned, carefully developed, and exists in a way that the CEO and marketing executives would like it to.

But not everything is within the company's control. And sometimes, it's those events and occurrences that are outside the company's control that tend to impact their brands the most.

Remember, because the true definition of "brand" is how a company is perceived, it doesn't always matter how the company would like to be perceived. Brands can take on a life of their own. They can be defined by customers' actions, PR snafus, employee misconduct, or tragic disasters.

The list goes on and on, but a few classic examples of good brands being redefined in a negative light stand out.

TWA

DISASTER STRIKES

TWA (Trans World Airlines) experienced a terrible tragedy and a branding nightmare, when they lost TWA Flight 800. In 1996, TWA was seventy-one years old. They were a large airline, based in the United States, and quite successful. They were one of the largest domestic airlines, and as far as airlines go, had a positive relationship with most of their customers. By all accounts, this was a strong brand.

But with one flight, the TWA brand would be changed forever. In what is still the third deadliest aviation accident in U.S. history, Flight 800 crashed into the Atlantic Ocean less than twenty minutes after takeoff, killing all 230 people on board.

The accident came to define the airline. Major news stories have a tendency to do that. And the company was never the same, eventually being bought out and merged with American Airlines.

To this day, when most people hear "TWA," they immediately think of that one tragic flight. That's not a good image for an airline.

bp

ACCIDENTAL BRANDING

BP, or British Petroleum, is a large multi-national gas and energy company based in London. They're the fourth largest company in the world, with operations in over eighty countries worldwide. They spend a great deal of time and energy on global branding. Even the way most people know the company, BP, is part of the plan.

They want you to call them BP, not British Petroleum. They want you to know that they spend a great deal of money on renewable energy. But even so, when you first encountered BP above, and you read it aloud in your head, you probably immediately thought of one thing.

The BP Oil Spill, or the Deepwater Horizon Oil Spill as it's come to be known, is the largest accidental marine oil spill in the history of the petroleum industry. It dominated the news for months, destroyed a great deal of wildlife in the Gulf of Mexico, and caused billions of dollars worth of damage to America's Gulf Coast.

It was an accident that probably could have been avoided, and one that has come to define BP's brand.

In an industry that's already reviled by many people, one that constantly takes it on the chin for being dirty, greedy, and bad for the environment, an event like this can be devastating. Especially after you spent millions of dollars trying to convince people that you're dedicated to being "green."

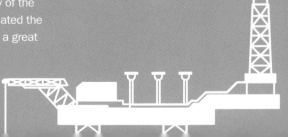

FAST FOOD ACTIVISM

A recent instance of negative branding is the great Chic-fil-A marketing disaster of 2012. Chic-fil-A is an American fast food chain based outside of Atlanta, which has been around since 1946. In recent years, the company has experienced stronger than average growth, helped in part by a fun advertising campaign, featuring cows telling people to "Eat Mor Chikin."

Starting in 2011, the company took a stand, albeit a more private one, against same-sex marriage. Donating to groups opposing the issue, the company kept out of the mainstream media. Then, in the spring of 2012, the company's CEO stepped out from behind the curtain and officially made it known that Chic-fil-A was against same-sex marriage. An uproar ensued.

The purpose of this book is not to make a stand, therefore I'll avoid it as much as possible.

But let's be honest; it's not in a marketer's best interest to have half of the country hate what your company stands for.

Now, you can't mention Chic-fil-A without thinking about their same-sex marriage stance. It defines the brand.

THE FIRST PART OF ANY GOOD MARKETING PLAN

The term "brand" comes from the Old Norse *brandr,* meaning to burn. It literally meant to burn your mark, or symbol, onto a product to indicate that it's yours. Think of cattle. Farmers would brand their cattle to mark them as their own. The marks on cows would tell other farmers to stay away. It's a way of telling other people that this group of cattle is yours.

This "mark" is the beginning of your "marketing plan." It will come to define who you are, what you do, and what your readers will expect of you.

And once you have a strong brand in place, it will make everything else that you do easier.

You'll be established in your market, field, or niche, and be seen by others as an authority.

BRANDING FOR BLOGGERS

Now that we've established what a brand is and introduced the idea of branding as the art of defining and controlling that brand, it's time to take the next step. Up until now I've talked about large companies. Sure, it's easy to talk about the brands of such well-known companies as Apple, BP, TWA, and Chic-fil-A. But how does that relate to you, the blogger?

Bloggers have brands. Blogs have brands. At least the successful ones do. And if you want to be a successful blogger, however you define success, it's up to you to define your brand, establish it in the hearts and minds of your readers, and use it to grow.

Some of the most successful blogs in the world have brands that many people in the blogosphere are very familiar with. Consider the top ten most popular blogs by monthly visits.

Your brand will be how people know you. It will help you distinguish who you are, and stand out from the crowd. In a world where 54,000 new blogs are started each and every day, those blogs that succeed will be the ones that have a well thought out marketing plan. And your brand is the first part of your marketing plan.

Many bloggers that I speak with think of a brand as a logo. Sure, a logo is part of your brand, but it's not the definition. Others tell me it's the theme, or design of their blog. Again, that's a part of it, but not the whole thing.

Your brand is larger than that. It's the experience that people have when they read, share, or interact in some way with your blog. It can go beyond what's actually included on the pages of your blog, and it spills over into social media channels, articles, sites, books, the products and services you sell, and anywhere else that you make your mark. Your brand becomes you, and vice versa.

Your brand will come to define who you are. Your readers will know exactly what to expect from you, because your brand tells them. New readers will get to know you through your brand. It will help you drive new visitors to your blog and earn money.

Source: The eBusiness Knowledgebase (eBizMBA.com)

Huffington Post
TMZ
Business Insider
Engadget
Perez Hilton
Gizmodo
Tech Crunch
Gawker
Lifehacker

0   20   40   60
November 2012: Blog Visits/Million

HOW DO YOU DEFINE SUCCESS?

As a blogger myself, I know that different bloggers define success very differently. Many bloggers start for personal reasons. Maybe they want to catalog a specific journey in their lives, such as the birth of their first child or the remodeling of their home. Maybe they're picking up a new hobby or starting a new quest. Maybe they feel that their opinion in a certain area is one that needs to be shared, heard, or included.

Other blogs are started for "professional" reasons. I define professional reasons as having a financial goal. Either the blog is intended to produce revenue, lead to a new revenue stream such as book or product sales, or lead to new or advanced career opportunities for the blogger.

And it's true that many of our "personal" bloggers will graduate to the "professional" category before too long. They enjoy the experience of blogging, develop a small following, and want to take their blog to the next level.

So wherever you are now, this book will focus on where you want to go next. Success can mean increased visitors, new subscribers, more monthly page views, more sales, more ads, or more money. It can be a combination of all these things. It's up to you to define what success looks like for your blog. It's my hope that the tips and techniques that will follow will help you get there.

BLASTOFF

In the chapters that follow, you'll learn from a variety of experts. Some will be experts on branding and marketing, aiming to transfer their knowledge of the marketing world to the specifics of blogging. Some will be bloggers who have identified the necessity of a strong brand and used their own brands to achieve success.

I have one foot squarely on both sides. As a marketer, I work day in and day out to learn all that I can about branding, reaching consumers, and communicating in the digital age. As a blogger, I use my knowledge of marketing to try to reach new readers, wider audiences, and sell my services.

Many bloggers, like many small business owners who don't come from a background similar to mine, struggle to identify as marketers. You may see yourself as an artist, a writer, a parent, a teacher, or something else entirely. Marketing is a strange and foreign world to you, maybe one that you've never taken the time to understand.

That's a line that you need to cross.

And it's a lot easier than you might expect it to be.

The goal of this book is to help you cross the line.

We'll break down the basics of branding as it relates to bloggers.

We'll identify tried-and-true techniques that you can use to define your brand, grow your brand, and use your brand to your advantage.

The book is divided into three chapters, each containing a number of sections centered around a core theme. The first chapter, "Defining Your Brand," covers the many ways you can establish your brand online, and help to convey the message to your readers about who you are and what you stand for. The second chapter, "Growing Your Brand," details a variety of ways you can grow the reach of your blog once readers are familiar with your site. The third and final chapter, "Using Your Brand," is all about the revenue opportunities that exist once you've established your brand.

You'll learn how your logo, domain name, and color scheme can come to mean much more than you think. How the structure of your blog and the length of your posts can help to define who you are. What your writing style tells your readers. How networking with other bloggers and communicating with your readers outside the "walls" of your blog can help establish your expertise in a given field. And how you can use all of these things, as part of a larger strategy, to achieve the kind of success that you desire—whether that means making money selling ads, writing a book, getting a job, or raising money to support a cause.

No one knows you as well as you. By the end of this book, you'll have the skills and the confidence to define yourself to the world through your blog.

Off we go!

DEFINING YOUR BRAND

The first step
in creating a strong brand is deciding what you want that brand to be.

In all likelihood, even if you haven't given this much thought, you already have the makings of a brand. It's up to you whether or not you want to build on what you already have or start anew, with a fresh branding strategy.

Defining your brand is a process that takes time for the blogger who's just now considering their brand. It requires you to spend some time thinking about your goals as a blogger, and how you want your readers to see you, read your posts, and interact with your blog.

How do you want your readers to see you?

Do you want them to see you as an expert in your field? Do you want them to contact you for advice? Do you want them to laugh?

In the sections that follow, you'll learn how all of the different aspects of your blog go into defining your brand to the world. And yes, we want you to think that big. The world is your audience.

You'll learn about naming your blog or company, choosing a domain name and a design that fits, defining your writing style and sticking to it, using different post lengths and frequency, and developing the supporting pages around your blog to give visitors the best possible experience when they come to your blog.

This first chapter is the most important. Once we've defined your brand, we'll lead you on the path of growing that brand and using it to drive the kind of traffic and income you dream about.

WHY ARE THEY READING?

To start with, ask yourself one simple question: "Why are people reading my blog?" The answer to that question will begin to lead you toward an idea of what your brand will be. It will help you to define your goals. It will tell you who you're writing for. And it will give you a pretty clear picture of what you're writing about.

How do you know the answer? That can be a bit harder to figure out, especially if you're just starting out or if you've yet to amass a great deal of readers. But take a look at your posts. Take a look at other blogs on similar topics. What makes you *different?*

Maybe people are reading your blog because they're interested in the same area as you. But that's not all. What else about your blog keeps them interested? Is it the way you write? Is it the amount of knowledge you have on a particular topic? Is it humor?

Whatever it is, it's important that you capture it and use it to help you define your brand and your blog moving forward.

Take a look at what good branding can do: Michela Chiucini (www.*webislove*.com) has one of those blogs you just want to stay on for hours at a time. No wonder, as one area she specializes in is blog design. Chiucini is a world-renowned web designer based out of Tuscany who has an extensive portfolio that includes Bigodino, Esn Card, and Napa, among others. "A blogger must first find her/his niche and define the audience," she says. With this in mind, she or he can start to define the brand: the tone of voice, the level of engagement expected, the design, the style, the logo, the content, and everything else that will make up the brand. Every aspect will contribute to define the brand of the blogger.

And yes, it's that large of a scale that we're dealing with here. People who are new to branding will be surprised at just how much goes into a successful brand. But think again about the large companies that have worked long and hard to brand themselves.

Think about Apple. What goes into branding Apple? Everything you see and hear from them, from the commercials on television to the billboards on the street, from the design of their retail stores to the design of their products, from the CEO giving a presentation on stage at a product launch to the genius selling you your new iPhone—they're all part of their brand. If any of those things did not follow or contribute to the brand, it would stand out. It would change the user experience for anyone who purchases or uses Apple products. And Apple, driven by perhaps one of the greatest branding experts of all time, the late Steve Jobs, just could not afford that.

So that's what branding is all about: creating an online personality for your blog that's identifiable to your readers.

Joe Pulizzi, co-author of *Managing Content Marketing,* believes it's helpful to visualize your ideal reader when brand strategizing. "Try putting the reader first. Then build an audience persona—a real-world idea of what your ideal reader might look like, and write to that."

Think of branding the way you think of a person's style. When we talk about "branding," we're really talking about making everything in your blog match. Not that you have to have only one font or color, but that the mood and personality of every part of your blog is identifiable as your brand. Branding is important for bloggers to learn about and understand because, face it, with so many blogs out there, and new ones popping up each hour, you need to make yourself stand out from the pack. Every part of your blog, from the posts written to the logo you create, will come to define your brand.

When most bloggers are just starting out, the idea of branding is simply not on their minds.

Depending on the field that you're in and the education you've pursued, you probably don't know much about what branding is, let alone why it might be an important part of running a successful blog.

The first focus is always on just getting started. And really, that's not a bad place to start.

According to Zac Johnson, successful blogger and author of *Blogging Tips: Confessions of a Six Figure Blogger*, "The best way to get started in the world of blogging is to actually get started. Don't worry about spending a ton of money on guides or consulting with gurus. You can easily get set up with your own domain name and hosting for only a few dollars a month. It's much more effective to learn everything as you walk through the process than trying to read everything you can about blogging and never actually getting started." As with anything, the adage "just do it" applies. It's important to really put yourself out there and establish your identity as a blogger before making any serious branding decisions. "You need to actually get started and learn through your actions, successes, and failures," said Johnson. So first, prior to branding your blog, you must *start blogging*.

Thousands of blogs are started every day for a variety of different reasons. They can begin simply as an outlet to express oneself, a vehicle to further promote a business venture, or as a source of emotional release, allowing one to cope with the difficulties of daily life.

I've seen blogs about bringing a child into the world, blogs about building a new home, blogs about helping out in developing countries, and blogs about blogging. Basically, whatever topic you consider blogging about, chances are there's already a blog on that topic. A quick Google search will prove me right.

So why should I start blogging if there's already one (or many) blogs in my niche?

How can I ever expect to be successful?

That's where branding comes in. As I said before, and as I'll continue to bring up later in this book, your brand will help you stand out from the blogs in your niche and become a go-to source for many readers.

What are the worst branding mistakes you've seen?

As someone who works in the business opportunities market, the worst branding mistakes I've seen involve taglines which are simply unbelievable.

For example, "Make $1,893 a Day with NO Website" or "How To Make $1000 Daily The Lazy Way" are out-and-out lies.

Yes, people buy into the myths, but soon learn that they wasted their money on bogus schemes."

—Ros Gardner
Net Profits Today
netprofitstoday.com

Think about Starbucks. Were they the first place to offer fresh coffee on the go?

No. But they defined themselves in a way that was very different from the other companies that were already operating in that space. The goal was to take the appeal of a local coffee shop and turn it into a chain that could expand across the country.

So how did they do this? First, they set about creating a café look and feel, something that people who enjoyed coffee houses could identify with. The coffee had to be good. The atmosphere had to be hip. And the menu had to be distinct. Starbucks is a story of branding success. They took this vision and developed a now worldwide chain of coffee houses that look and feel like local places no matter where you are. They have become prime places for coffee lovers and fans all over the world. When you go into a Starbucks you know what to expect, because you're familiar with the brand, which took a lot of time and energy to build.

Let's take a look at a few bloggers who got started for different reasons but all found a level of success that they didn't expect. I'll keep referring back to these and other successful bloggers and branding experts throughout the book to give you a real-world picture of the advice provided.

Robin Callan, owner of Room Fu—Knockout Interiors and operator of the 2012 Homie-nominated blog Fu For Thought (*roomfu.com/blog*), explains how her blog started out as a marketing tool. But it never stopped growing.

"It started out purely as a way to market my design business, but it has taken on a life of its own," Callan says. "Blogging is an opportunity to show more of my design style than you might see in my portfolio, and it gives potential clients insight into my personality as well. Since chemistry is one of the most important elements of a working relationship between a designer and client, this is a unique way for us to have that feeling of connection before an initial consultation."

Emily Rapp, author of the powerful memoir *Poster Child* about her experience growing up with a prosthetic leg, started her blog for a completely different reason. Her blog, Little Seal (*ourlittleseal.wordpress.com*), about her son's terminal illness is lively, fresh, and free of self-pity. It was also on *Time* magazine's list of the 25 Best Blogs of 2012. Rapp's story reveals her undaunted spirit, a spirit that permeates every sentence she types. "My good friend Weber suggested that I start a blog in the weeks after Ronan was diagnosed," says Rapp. "Initially I was writing in it every day, and it gave me a great sense of peace and purpose in the midst of a completely chaotic situation. It also helped shape the voice

and style of a full-length book project. The book, called *The Still Point of the Turning World,* is published by Penguin Press."

Famed freelancer, blogger, Super Affiliate marketer, and instructional author Ros Gardner (*netprofitstoday.com*) says you shouldn't start a blog on a topic just because you think it'll sell. Instead, follow your passion. "Blog about a topic that truly interests you," Gardner says. "It's extremely difficult to discuss a topic one knows nothing about, which makes it impossible to make honest, in-depth product recommendations—and surfers don't buy from sites where lack of knowledge and experience is obvious." Of course, this is time consuming, so

make sure you have the commitment in addition to the interest. "It takes time and energy to create a content-rich site that's popular and is trusted by visitors. If you can't fathom writing about a particular topic in a year from now, you should consider choosing another topic," Gardner says.

Carefully choosing your content area based on your own knowledge and experience is a crucial step in the development of any high-traffic blog.

GETTING STARTED

Once you've decided you want to start a blog, and you've chosen a topic you're truly passionate about, the next step is to define your brand. According to Pamela Wilson (*bigbrandsystems.com*), award-winning graphic designer and marketing consultant, this is a two-step process that happens internally first, and then externally.

The first part comes from carefully considering what your blog is, and what you want it to do. "First, you have to do some internal work to get clear about who you're trying to reach, the tone you'd like to strike, and the message you'd like to communicate," she says. "Getting clear about who you're trying to reach means understanding who your ideal reader is. You want to have a vivid image of this person in your mind: what is their gender, age, education level? Many people resist this step, saying, 'I want to appeal to everyone!'"

But we know what happens when you try to please all the people all the time; you lose sight of your own vision and you end up appealing to no one.

"Unfortunately, when you try to appeal to a broad audience, you tend to water down your brand to the point that it makes no impact," Wilson says. "It works better when you know exactly who your ideal customer is, and you speak in a way that will appeal to that person. Once you know who it is you want to reach, striking the right tone becomes easier," she says. Wilson advises considering three factors in how your ideal customer communicates.

1. How do they speak about their challenges? What words and phrases do they use? How would they describe what it is they see and go through on a daily basis and how can you relate to them?

2. How much time do they have on their hands? Are they readers, skimmers, or would they prefer to watch video? How in depth do they want you to go on any particular topic and how much of what they're looking for is fact versus opinion?

3. What else do they consume? What magazines, websites, and entertainment are popular among the group you're trying to reach?

Understanding your audience is an important factor in determining how you want them to experience your blog and interact with its content. "Instead of thinking of your audience as a collection of people," say Andrew Boer and Andrew Eisner ("The Andrews"), President and COO respectively of the content marketing agency Movable Media (*movablemedia.com*), "think of them as a brand. What do they stand for? Could you give them a name?

Would they self-identify with it?" Asking these fundamental questions will provide you with a better perspective on the relationship between your brand and your audience and how the two influence each other.

Think about Walmart. What does Walmart stand for? We can all remember their "Everyday Low Prices" slogan. The brand is all about giving people a place to shop for anything and everything that they need at the lowest prices around. Walmart defines their audience, albeit a rather large one, as shoppers who are in need of or looking for a bargain. They know what they want and they want it to be inexpensive. They care about convenience, and they'd like to get everything they need in one trip from one supplier.

Using this definition of their audience, they know who they're not trying to appeal to. They know they're not appealing to the fashion aficionados who shop at brand name designer stores and go into storefront after storefront, hunting down the item that fits their style the best, even if it means trying on many different items. They know they're not going after the early-adopting tech crowd who don't care about price as long as they can get their hands on the latest and trendiest gadget before all of their friends.

Knowing who you're trying to reach is important. But even more vitally, it tells you who you're *not* trying to reach. And the beginnings of a brand start to form around both of those ideas. It will help you decide what and how to write about a topic, and what you can leave out altogether.

Even before you've built an audience, you have to make some decisions about how you'll present yourself. "After you gather some readers around your work, you can base your information on interactions with them. Once you understand your audience and have decided on a tone, you should develop an overall message. This is a phrase, or a sentence or two, that remind you of the purpose of your blog," says Pamela Wilson.

This overall message, which is known in the marketing world as a *mission statement* or *brand promise,* is the foundation upon which every successful blog is built. Wilson can attest to its importance to the success of her own blog. "In the case of my blog, Big Brand System, I help small business owners learn about marketing and design so they can promote their businesses themselves," she says. "The overriding message behind all my posts is 'you can do this.' I don't write about problems without offering a solution. I always write with the goal of empowering the reader to do more for their business. Keeping this overall message in mind has helped my blog stay focused and consistent through the years."

It's necessary to constantly revisit your mission statement to ensure your blog hasn't lost focus and you're staying true to the goals you set out for it. However, just like a blog, a mission statement shouldn't be set in stone and should be altered if you find your brand changing over time.

So that's the internal work you have to do first. Once you've got that all settled, you can start looking at how to express your brand externally, "through your choice of blog name and tagline, domain name, and website style," Wilson says. "Remember: the internal sets the stage for the external. It's not sexy to do the internal work, but the external expression of your brand won't be successful unless you've got the internal components right." Also, making sure your internal and external components mesh is vital to growing your brand and increasing your blog viewership. If they don't, your approach will be inconsistent and your reader will have trouble trusting you.

So how do we take the internal work and begin to create the external?

Let's find out.

WHAT'S IN A NAME?

The first of these external steps is to choose a name. But unlike naming your baby, naming your blog also involves choosing a domain name. You may come up with the most clever name for your blog about decorating, say, "Apartment Therapy" or "Design Sponge," and get the whole site designed around that name, only to find out those domains are already taken. (As they are, in fact, by a couple of great blogs on interior design and décor).

Your starting point should be to brainstorm a list of potential domain names that pertain to your topic, maybe with a couple of creative friends. You can then upload your list of names using the bulk upload tool on a number of domain purchasing and management services such as GoDaddy, Register.com, or Network Solutions to see which are available.

If you can't think of any good names, *Dot-o-nator.com* is a useful website which generates domain name ideas and word combinations. Aim for a name that will tell the reader something about the content, but which will also tell the reader something about the style. For example, Paris Imperfect, a blog by the displaced New Yorker Sion Dayson, is about living in Paris and about being a writer. The name captures all of that and lets the reader know there's also a certain amount of self-deprecating humor in the blogger's point of view.

There are a couple of different schools of thought when it comes to selecting a domain name and naming your blog. In the past, many people thought it was okay to name your blog something completely different from your domain name. For example, your domain name might be your name, *joeschmo.com*, even if the name of your blog was "All About Eggs." The two don't relate, but as long as people understood where to go to find All About Eggs, who cares?

In fact, using your name as a domain is a very popular practice, even if the name of your blog is different.

But today's websites and blogs become defined by their URLs. The name of the blog and the domain name become the same thing, and when there's a disconnect, it can be confusing for the reader. So my recommendation is always to choose a domain name that matches the name of your blog. And you'll find that most of the blogs we've profiled in this book follow that practice.

So consider naming your blog, and finding an available domain name, both one and the same. Domain names can be hard to come by, and the one you want may not always be available to you. So be prepared to be creative, or to do a little extra work to get the name you want.

Michela Chiucini, whose *Web Is Love* blog has a terrifically compelling design, says that you need to really think hard about your domain before buying it. "The domain is a tricky one; it requires a bit of luck and/or a bit of creativity. In general it should be easy to remember and related to the content. In that way the audience will remember it." Once you've come up with a few names, you must check and see if the domains have been taken by others.

To do this, you have to first go to a reputable domain marketplace that aggregates a wide variety of auctions, such as *domaintools.com* or *sedo.com*. The next step is to type each of the domain names into your search bar and see what comes up. Break the pages you find into four distinct categories based on their characteristics, including pages that are non-existent, pages that are under construction, pages that are links to other sites (often for lead generation), and real businesses.

After identifying the status of each page, you can use the contact information provided to try and get in touch with the domain owners to see if the name is for sale. Some sites will embed a contact link for those who are interested in purchasing the domain name (this typically makes negotiations easier, but more on this later). If no contact information is provided or the page is dead (this doesn't necessarily mean no one owns it, just that it hasn't been maintained), you can search the

Internet Archive (*archive.org/web/web.php*) to find old pages and contact details or do a WHOIS search on any reputable query database for domain registration information.

Tracking down the owners and communicating with them can at times be a slow and arduous process. However, your patience and persistence may be rewarded if you end up purchasing a strong domain name for little money. Sometimes it's next to impossible to locate the owner, in which case you're probably best served to just move on to other options.

If it's your first time purchasing a domain name, contact the owners directly. If instead you've purchased a string of domains and your contact information and business history can be found easily through a Web search, you may want to think about masking your identity by using one of a number of techniques. This is because the owners are more likely to quote you a higher price if you have a history of buying up domain names. One quick and easy way to mask is to create an anonymous Yahoo! or Gmail account without any of your contact information listed. If you don't, the domain owners are more likely to think you're a scammer and may be hesitant to sell to you.

If you're willing to pay for this service, you can use a website that offers masking capabilities, such as *networksolutions.com,* or you can hire a small law or PR firm with a website and use a Web address that they create. This ensures that the domain owners will think you're a real person but won't necessarily try to highball you in pricing negotiations. When making first contact with the owners, it's important to remember not to make an initial offer before determining if the domain is for sale or not. Once you enter into negotiations, have a valuation in mind, since you're unlikely to have any point of comparison to determine what you should pay.

In the end, naming your blog shouldn't be all that much of a hassle. It's the first step in branding, as the name that you choose will be synonymous with your brand in the long run (we hope). But it's not the be-all and end-all of defining your brand. So don't get all your hopes set on one name only to find out you have to settle for something else down the road.

Be flexible. And be creative. That's what makes a strong name easy to find.

DESIGN

Launching your blog will require a certain amount of design. Maybe you already have a design on your blog, or maybe you've started blogging without worrying too much about the way that your site looks. What you'll learn is that everything about your blog contributes to the way people view it. The length of your posts, the font that you use, the colors, the pages, and the elements on the top and side of each page will all impact the way your blog looks.

Design has a lot to do with your brand. It should create a visual impact on the readers who frequent your site. Your most avid readers will feel at home there. Designs can be very simple or very complex, but the key is consistency.

In the sections that follow, we'll talk about the design of several key elements on your blog. The design aspect of your site is one that should be considered carefully. Most blogging platforms will allow non-programmers or non-designers to use simple tools to affect the way a blog looks and feels. But many of the most successful bloggers have realized the need for a more advanced level of expertise in design. If you're not familiar with Web design or have little experience with what makes a design successful, I recommend that you hire or consult a professional for many of the elements mentioned in this section. A professional will bring a certain amount of experience and familiarity to the table that will help the overall appeal of your blog.

LOGO

The first part of your blog's design on which you should focus is the logo. The logo should be something that will capture the essence of your brand and what you're trying to communicate to your readers, just the way your name will.

Think, for example, of how the seemingly timeless Coca-Cola logo has become synonymous with the very product the company is advertising and the way it's viewed by the consumer. You don't need to listen to a sales pitch for the product. You don't need to see someone drinking a can of Coke. You don't even need to see the name of the company spelled out separately. When you see the logo, you think Coca-Cola. You think of all the times you've seen or interacted with the product. It's a brand, above all else.

Your logo should be simple. Most blogs use the name of the blog in the logo. It should be something that's readily recognizable and easy to duplicate. Your logo will become the key image that you can use and share anywhere on the Web to direct people to your blog. Eventually, when people see your logo they should know who you are and that the content associated with your logo is yours and yours alone.

Your logo is often the first thing that appears at the top of your blog, in an element we refer to as the website header.

According to Pamela Wilson, "This is the first thing your visitors see when they land on your site, and it sets the tone for everything that follows. It's important, obviously, that your site header state the name of your blog. You want to reassure your visitors that they're in the right place."

"Beyond that," she says, "I'm a proponent of keeping things simple. State your blog name with a unique font (find a free one at *fontsquirrel.com*) and you'll be done. Apply a color or two as a bonus, and it will look even better. And while it's important to carefully choose a header, remember that it may change over time," Wilson says.

Keeping your mission statement in mind when developing your blog's visual identity is crucial in order to ensure that the two form a united front for your brand. This is, of course, subject to change as your blog grows and your goals evolve. "Later, as you develop a relationship with your readers, you can spring for a more elaborate header design. It's usually better to wait until you truly understand your audience before you invest too much in a website header," Wilson adds.

There are some common mistakes to avoid when designing your logo. These mistakes are made every day by large companies, so don't feel bad if you've already made some yourself. Experimenting with your logo and modifying it over time is common. But when you get something you're happy with and appeals to your readers, keep it consistent. This will make you more recognizable than someone who is constantly changing their look.

1 The first mistake is to copy another logo. It might be easy to choose a well-known company and assume they know something about logo design that you don't. Copying a certain look might make you think you've tapped into some expertise and allow you to achieve the same level of success. But one of the keys of a strong logo design is uniqueness. Express yourself and who you are instead of trying to duplicate someone else's success.

Two classic examples of similar logos (whether intentional or not).

2 Another common mistake is the use of stock art. I see this all the time. Once again, elements of a logo should be unique. If you use a piece of art that everyone's seen on other sites, it makes your logo look cheap and amateurish.

Some of the most used stock logos (birds, globes, arrows, stars, and leaves) can make your logo look generic and ordinary.

GOBIERNO DE CHILE

After a 2010 election, the Chilean government unveiled a logo for the transitional government which is a perfect example of an overly complex logo design.

Apple computers used a rainbow of colors in their logo which was used from 1976 to 1998. It was redesigned to a monochromatic version that is still used today.

[3] A third common mistake to avoid is creating a logo that is too complex. Complexity is something to avoid in all aspects of your blog's design. Complexity makes information more difficult to process, and it makes recreating a design that much more difficult. Unique does not mean complex. You can achieve uniqueness in a simple design, and that is what you should aim for at all times.

[4] The final mistake that you want to avoid is the use of too many colors or too many fonts. Your logo's color will come to define the colors that readers will associate with your brand. One or two colors is plenty, and reduces confusion. The same goes for the fonts that you choose. Use a font that effectively communicates the style of your blog, and don't try to complicate things with a combination of multiple fonts.

A good idea for coming up with a final logo design (or any design for that matter) is to come up with what you think works the best and try it out.

Gather a group, preferably made up of the same type of people as your audience (as defined by you in the previous section). Present them with several different variations of the logo that you've come up with. To keep things interesting, throw in some logos that are different than what you've chosen. Ask them for feedback. What do they like? What don't they like? What kinds of emotions do they have when they see your logo?

The feedback that you get from this focus group style interaction will tell you how people will see your logo.

A key to creating something that appeals to your audience is to get real, honest feedback from the audience you seek.

You're not designing for yourself, you're designing for your readers.

What do they expect to see, or what do they associate the logo with?

Once you settle on a logo, designing the pages of your blog around that logo becomes key.

PAGE DESIGN

The best blogs have a professional design. But it's not always necessary. Much of how your blog looks will depend on the style and topic that you're writing about and the type of people it will attract. Some of the most successful blogs in the world look simple.

You wouldn't know by looking at them how much time and energy has gone into creating something so bland.

Once you have the name, you've bought the domain, and you've designed a logo, it's time to design the entire blog. Look at any successful blog and you'll notice that it has a look and feel that is consistent throughout the site. Everything from the colors, to the fonts, to the size of the text, to the use of graphics affects the way that your blog looks.

Michela Chiucini advises that a blogger should hire a designer unless he or she is design-savvy. "If the blog will become popular, the logo will be popular as well. If the blogger is not a designer, it's better to hire a professional that can do it. Websites like *dribbble.com* are full of professional logo designers," she says.

Robin Callan opted for this approach. "My blog is part of my design business website, so its look and feel is consistent with the rest of my site," Callan says. "I can't take credit for it though; I was smart enough to hire Austin web designer Karen Barry to do the heavy lifting where the design is concerned! But the overall idea was to use color and imagery that projected 'modern' and 'fun,' with plenty of 'Keep Austin Weird'-ness thrown into the mix. That's the prevailing state of mind here in our capital city and I'm proud to be part of that," she says.

How should you choose the predominant elements of your blog's background and graphics?

Let's delve into design a little bit deeper.

FIVE THôT (getthefive.com)

Design Milk (design-milk.com)

Fast Co. Design (fastcodesign.com)

The Selby (theselby.com)

Examples of well-designed page layouts for blogs and websites.

COLORS

Pamela Wilson explains it very simply: "When it comes to colors, my advice is to choose two colors to emphasize on your site. Don't count black type or your white background. Simply add these two main colors to your page, and emphasize them over and over throughout your site elements like subheads, graphics, and link colors."

So what colors should you choose?

Color choice is important in any blog design. It's a form of non-verbal communication that says a lot about who you are and what you're trying to convey. Think about the colors of some of the world's most famous brands. Coca-Cola's red, Apple's white, Facebook's blue, Best Buy's yellow, Yahoo!'s purple. They all have a dominant color that's easily recognizable and identifiable. That's what you want, something that says something about you.

Colors bring with them certain emotions. For example, red is often associated with passion and excitement. Blue is often associated with trust and stability, peace and tranquility. Yellow is often associated with liveliness and energy. Orange is associated with ingenuity and creativity. Purple is associated with nobility and wealth. Green is associated with harmony and life.

The color you choose to be your dominant color should have something to do with the way you want your readers to feel when they first land on your website. A blog with a green dominant color will be viewed differently than if the same blog had used red.

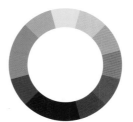

Once you choose a *primary* color, refer to a color wheel to help you develop *secondary* colors around the dominant one. It's not just designers who think there are colors that naturally go with one another. We all think this, though our feelings may be a little more subconscious than a designer's.

The color wheel.

The color wheel will guide you to colors that go together. Opposing colors on the color wheel are referred to as *complementary* colors. Adjacent colors on the color wheel are referred to as *analogous* colors. These two types of color combinations are seen in the natural world, and are easily recognized by most people who view them on the Web or in any other type of design. Don't go against the grain here or you're more likely to create a combination of colors that's difficult to look at for any extended period of time. That's not a winning strategy for a blogger who's trying to draw in first-time visitors and create return readers.

Primary colors.

Secondary colors.

Complementary color example.

Analogous color example.

FONTS

Beyond that, what kind of font do you want? Comic Sans will give a very different feeling than Baskerville. Try out a few different fonts before settling on the one that best expresses your brand. "I recommend choosing no more than two font families to display on your site. Find two families that have a variety of weights, so you can use regular, italic, and bold versions of your fonts for maximum versatility," says Pamela Wilson.

Even if we don't think about fonts when we're looking at a website, the font choice is still impacting the way we view content. We've all tried to read something only to be frustrated by the way it looks. Compare the choice of fonts on many popular blogs and you'll

most likely find that some are easier to read than others.

Check out a website like *MyFonts.com* to find out what kinds of fonts you like or don't like. Here you can search for fonts that are most popular, fonts that elicit specific emotions and feelings in the reader, fonts that relate to one another, and fonts that people are using most often.

Once again, the key to choosing a font is simplicity and consistency. Pick something that is simple enough that it has broad appeal. And use it exclusively. If your font changes from one post to another, it will most likely confuse readers. The last thing you want to do when building a successful brand is to confuse people by deviating from what they've come to expect.

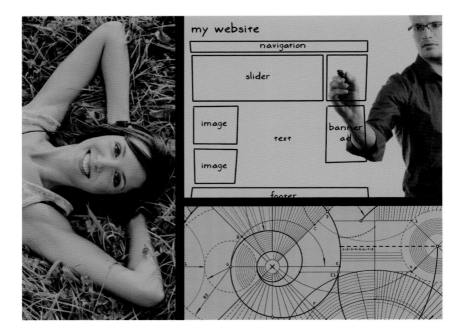

LAYOUT

The layout of your blog must also be considered, as it's often just as important in communicating with your viewers as the content you generate. What kind of layout will fit your brand? Would a newspaper format work better or should you use a single column? Will separate tabs along the upper third of the main page represent your blog's different sections? What kinds of graphics will you use, how will they be organized, and where will they be displayed? When considering the design, the most important factor to keep in mind is that you have a ton of choices. Don't just go with the obvious, but play with your layout, and experiment until you get a design that really expresses your brand.

Again, listen to the advice of design expert Michela Chiucini: "When it comes to blog design, the aspects related to easy reading and interaction are fundamental. You want people to stay on your website, so be careful with cluttered interfaces and too much content at a glance. A touch of originality plays an important role as well; it allows the blog to stand out and to be remembered and recognized. In a nutshell, I'd say go with a layout for its simplicity and originality." Too frequently, beginning bloggers think they have to attract traffic to their site with overly elaborate designs and a glut of content. However, this can often drive people away from a site. Many times the best approach is a clean, deliberate design with an easy-to-use interface, and a clear, concise message.

Chiucini emphasizes the importance of knowing your audience and having your design reflect what the viewer is looking to get out of your blog. "With my own blog design, I went through some revisions and simplifications. I knew my audience would be Web design peeps, so the goal was a simple and flexible design that could be customized with the image of the last post, just enough to not become boring," she says. I see many blogs put together from one day to another.

For new bloggers, my suggestion is to try to reflect the brand through design and to look for a simple, but meaningful design.

Responsiveness is important as well, as many people today read blogs from their Smartphones.

And while we're on the subject, certain aspects of your blog's design will have to be viewable on both desktop computers and mobile devices. We'll talk a little bit more in depth about mobile devices near the end of the book, but for now we should point out that you have to keep mobile viewing in mind when designing all aspects of your blog. Always remember to double check the way your blog looks on a tablet and Smartphone. If you don't have one of each, borrow them from a friend.

One of the worst mistakes you can make in today's digital age, an age in which a higher percentage of people are consuming content online with phones and tablets as opposed to traditional desktop computers, is to fail to consider the way your blog looks on one of these popular devices.

PERSONALITY AND WRITING STYLE

Personality and writing style are two intertwined elements that people don't spend too much time thinking about. The best writers in the world have perfected a style that is completely theirs. Their readers can tell that this is the author they know and love just by the way something is written. And that's the goal with your blog: find a writing style that's completely yours.

The best writing for your blog is your own style. That may sound simple, or it may sound impossible. The trick is to sound exactly like yourself—your own most natural, genuine self. And that can take some time to get the hang of.

Ros Gardner, whose popular blog *RosalindGardner.com* is a great model of how to be authentic in your writing style, says it wasn't always so easy for her. "When I started publishing online, I had visions of people being hugely critical of my work, so I strove to make every word perfect. As a result, I sounded stilted and contrived. However, the criticism I feared never came up. It would seem that by virtue of the fact that you're willing to put yourself out there, especially when your motive is to help and share with others, brings out the best in people. With my readers' encouragement, I overcame the oppression of perfectionism and started to write as I thought and spoke. A couple of years after I started publishing online, a woman I met at a conference said, 'You speak exactly as you write; I would have known you anywhere.' It's one of the greatest compliments I've ever known. So, my advice is just to be yourself and have fun."

And the fear of perfection comes up time and time again when I talked to bloggers for this book. It takes a great deal of faith to put your thoughts and opinions, sometimes your entire life, out there for all the world to see. As human beings, we spend so much time trying to protect ourselves, often going to great lengths to try to retain some bit of privacy from the world.

But bloggers are different. Blogging is a step into the public world, even if it's done from behind the keyboard.

And with that step, you have to be prepared to get negative feedback or criticism. It comes with the territory, and if you spend too much time trying to avoid it, you'll never really let your true self show, and you won't be able to reach your fullest potential.

When you write as yourself, as you would speak or write in any situation, you'll find that it comes naturally. It will make the entire blogging process simpler and smoother. You'll enjoy yourself and be better able to explain how you really feel.

Too often bloggers try to sound overly professional. They write in a way they wouldn't normally write, just to sound like an expert. All that does is make your writing come across as phony and not genuine. You'll not build any trust with your readers, who can go get the same bland facts from someone who might be a more credible expert.

In addition, trying to sound professional will make writing harder and blogging will feel like more of a job than an activity you enjoy. Running a successful blog already takes dedication, and if you don't enjoy the work, you'll find it very difficult to stay the course.

Liz Strauss agrees about the importance of retaining your own voice. Strauss is the CEO and founder of SOBCon, author of *SuccessfulBlog.com,* and according to Connie Deiken of the *Huffington Post,* "one of the most thoughtful, prolific bloggers on the planet." Strauss says, "You are the only you. Use your voice. Your writing voice is the sound of your brand. You are your most powerful tool for connecting with readers. The sound of your voice places your words in our minds and hearts. It's the business of authenticity. We hear your voice, and we trust what you're saying."

So too does Robin Callan, who has adapted the approach to her entire interior design business. "The voice and tone of my blog sets it apart from other designers' blogs. People expect a practicing interior designer to be a little bit serious, maybe even a little snobby. Let's face it—interior design has been stuck-up for generations, so I use my blog as a tool to make design more approachable. Part of that effort is allowing a bit of snark and sarcasm to slip in every once in a while. At the end of the day, I absolutely want to gush over beautiful design, but if I see something on a TV decorating show that is butt-ugly, I'm going to call that crap out. Either way, I tell it like it is, and people who read my blog tell me all the time how much they appreciate that." Michela Chiucini also chimes in, adding: "Find your own voice, your own niche, your own style, and write original content. The Web needs that."

I love the way Robin and Michela use their blogs to make design more approachable. The blog becomes an outlet to relate to people.

I see this all the time in the blogo-sphere, and if you follow a number of blogs, you'll probably see it as well. The blogosphere is filled with strong opinions, quirky characters, big personalities, and at times even bigger jerks. It's a space that welcomes personality. It's a new form of journalism that's looking for the way you fit into the story. By putting more of yourself out there for people to see, you can build a rapport with your readers, who'll come to accept you and love you for saying what you have to say. That's what will keep them coming back time and time again.

While being interested in a topic is important, equally important is having some expertise in the subject. This doesn't mean you have to hold a PhD in agriculture in order to write a successful blog about your farm, but it does mean you should probably have a farm and/or know something about how to grow a good pumpkin.

"When you build a site around a topic about which you're knowledgeable and have credibility, or about which you're willing to learn, the result is improved conversion rates, increased sales, and ultimately, success," Ros Gardner says, adding this for incentive: "Every multi-millionaire I know (and I know many) started their business in a niche about which they were interested, knowledge-able, and even passionate."

"Don't be afraid to share your true per-spective," says Robin Callan. Readers relate to authenticity, and they're more loyal to blogs that aren't generic.

Bottom line, take the advice your mother has been giving you your whole life, and be yourself.

Traits of Effective Internet Writing

In her book, *The Secret to Writing a Successful and Outstanding Blog,* Liz Strauss emphasizes the importance of the blog's written style, with "6 +1 Traits of Effective Internet Writing."

1. Ideas

Ideas are the stuff of which messages are made. We look for them . . . wish for them. They're memorable, strong, and effective, or they're . . . not.

2. Organization

Ordering ideas logically is how we present ideas so that they make sense to others.

3. Voice

Voice is tone and style that is consciously chosen to suit the intended audience.

4. Word Choice

Word choice is finding the perfect word to convey a message in an authentic, rich, and precise fashion to elicit a response.

5. Sentence Fluency

Sentence fluency is making sentences work together so that the reading moves with pacing, flow, and rhythm.

6. Writing Conventions

Writing conventions are agreed-upon rules of writing. Punctuation, spelling, and grammar qualify—as do keywords, alt tags, and SEO.

7. Presentation

Presentation is the preparation of the written message in a way that draws readers to connect with the message on a personal level even before they begin to read. For a blog, presentation is when you hit "Publish" and the conversation begins.

None of these seven traits will be found in a text on rocket science, but all seven are critical to whether your text communicates. All quality writing has these traits.

POST LENGTH AND FREQUENCY

Beginning bloggers often want to know two things: how long should each post be, and how often should I post? The answer to both depends on the blog, and especially on the readers of the blog.

"Post length should be in response to your readers' lifestyles. If you're writing for an audience that has more time to read, you can write longer posts. If your audience is strapped for time, shorter posts are better. It's important to experiment: try a little of each style at first, and see what the response is. Throw in an occasional audio interview or video post, and see what kind of reaction you get. Your readers will tell you what they want by their comments, sharing activity on social media, and their emails to you," says Pamela Wilson.

In terms of frequency, before you even start a blog, you should ask yourself if you're really ready to commit. Nothing says "dead in the water" like a blog whose most recent post is dated a month ago. You should be able to post a minimum of a couple of times each month, according to Wilson. For many blogs, you'll have to post more frequently.

"If you can't commit to that, you shouldn't start blogging," says Wilson, who posts once every week, on Wednesdays, and starts thinking about the next week's post on Thursday. By following her lead, you'll stay constantly engaged with your blog, even when you're temporarily away from it. "People's attention spans are short, and less than two posts a month just won't make enough impact to build your audience," she says. "From a production standpoint, it's helpful to choose a specific day of the week to post, and work backward from that."

When thinking about frequency, consider the production schedule. "I aim for a three-day production schedule," Wilson says. "I write the headline and mind map the content on the first day, fill in the details on the second day, and look for an image and proofread it one last time on the third day." Regardless of how frequently you decide to post (perhaps you follow Wilson's lead and chose to blog every Wednesday), it's important to stick to a schedule so your viewers know when they can expect new content.

Breaking your schedule too often can lead to your audience losing trust in you and going elsewhere.

You'll find that all bloggers differ on the frequency with which they post, and the strategy they use to put their posts together. Some blogs post new content every day, the largest ones posting several times each day (usually this involves a team of writers). Some blogs post a couple of times per week. And still others, like Pamela, post once a week or less. The key, I'll stress once again, is consistency. Once you've established a

regular pattern, your readers will come to know and expect that pattern. Any deviation from the schedule might result in confusion.

It's helpful for all beginning bloggers to establish an editorial calendar, and fill it in with the dates, times, and tasks you plan to do going forward. Keep in mind that the calendar should not only include your blog-post production schedule, but also when you plan to read and respond to user comments, market your blog on Twitter, Facebook, and other social networks, and scrutinize your analytics and make the necessary adjustments to your site. It's equally important to allocate enough time for each item, so you won't end up feeling overwhelmed, and the quality of the content you produce or the R&D you put into posts won't suffer. Once you've gotten into a routine you're comfortable with, it'll soon become second nature to you, making it easier to remain productive and avoid writer's block. Your editorial calendar should keep you playing the roles of writer, marketer, and blog mechanic, at least until you hire someone to perform those services for you.

When you're just starting out, it's important to find a schedule that works for you, and time blocks that you think you'll be able to stick to. Don't overcommit yourself at the very beginning. It may be easy to write a lot when you're just starting out, because you haven't had a chance to say everything you know about your blog topic yet. But think about what it will feel like a year from now. How hard will you have to try to scrape together a new post? How often do you want to be creating new content, again and again?

And think about the types of posts you're going to write. Do they require a lot of research? Will you have to find and quote sources? Will you have to find other people to interview? Or will each post be quick and easy, something that just flows out of your own mind?

The answers to these questions will tell you how much time and energy will go into your writing before each post can go live, and it may steer you in one direction or another when it comes to post frequency.

Take a look at some of the other blogs in your niche. Do a quick Google search and start to read through a few of them. How often do they post? What types of posts are they writing? Use this as a guide (though you don't *ever* want to copy them exactly).

One particular technique that I advise, and that many a successful blogger employs, is to always have five or more well-written, timeless, publish-able posts saved in your drafts, so if

anything comes up last minute and you don't have time to write a new post, you can just set one of your prewritten ones to publish. Keep holidays, seasons, birthdays, and other events in mind, as they can be hectic times for you and your family. You may think you'll have the time to get everything done, and maybe you will, but life, as we all know, has a tendency to throw curveballs at us.

When creating posts to save as drafts, it obviously doesn't make sense to write about a current event that will be old news by the time the post goes live.

Instead, stick to topics that have real staying power and will retain a level of interest in the weeks and months to come, keeping the current issues and topics for your next few published posts. So if you feel like writing up a storm one day, by all means do so, but rather than clicking publish on four posts in a row in a given day, consider saving one or two for a later date when you're swamped or you have an emergency to attend to.

OTHER PAGES ON YOUR BLOG

In addition to your main blog page, where you'll do the majority of your writing, your blog will need some additional supporting pages in order to be successful. If you look at other popular blogs, you'll notice these more and more.

Let's go through a couple of the most important pages and how to use them to support your brand.

ABOUT PAGE

The About page is the first place people will look if they begin to follow your blog regularly. It's a page that will tell visitors who you are.

As readers of a blog, we want to feel connected to the people behind the content that we most like to consume. It's a natural thing we all experience. We don't want to take our advice from, get our facts from, or trust someone who is anonymous. We prefer to feel like we know the person behind the brand. And in that way, the person behind the brand becomes an essential piece of the brand.

All for Your Readers

The most successful Contact and About pages are actually about the reader, not the author.

You have an opportunity on your Contact page to demonstrate that you empathize with your reader's challenges and want to help them through the language you use when inviting them to get in touch.

And your About page can be mostly about them, their issues, and what kinds of solutions to those issues they'll find on your blog.

After you've established that you understand them and have help for them, then you can talk about why you're qualified to help.

You can also let visitors know how they can stay in contact with you on your About page: include a contact form, and consider adding social media icons so they can connect with you on whatever platforms you're active on.

—Pamela Wilson
Big Brand System
bigbrandsystem.com

Now, not everyone makes it easy to find out who they are. Many bloggers prefer to remain anonymous, or keep their blogging personalities separate from their personal lives (or even a separate professional life). And you may have a desire to keep these things separate as well.

There's no binding law here, but you picked up this book for advice, so I'll refrain from straddling the fence on this one. In my opinion, you should be as open as you can be about who you are and why you're worth listening to. The most successful bloggers are very open about their lives, their credentials, and their opinions.

The About page is a great place to showcase yourself in the best possible light. Include a headshot so people can put a face to your name. Write up a short bio that addresses who you are and why you write what you do.

This will establish trust and credibility with the reader.

Credibility is a major factor in developing a successful blog and one we'll address in greater detail later in this book.

CONTACT PAGE

The Contact page is another essential piece of your blog if you wish to grow it into one of the more successful blogs out there. One of the keys to successful blogging is giving your readers a way to interact with the blog. We'll discuss more about the difference between active and passive readers later, but for now let's focus on why you want to include a Contact page.

The Contact page gives your readers a way to get in touch with you, outside of the traditional comments section that follows each post. This gives them a way to reach out to the blogger directly. It creates a link from them to you, one that helps to establish your credibility by making you "real."

A Contact page should include an email address that people can use to get in touch with you or a contact form that automatically generates an email to you.

Many people are careful not to make their email address public at the risk of getting overwhelmed with spam. But a contact form allows you to stay in touch without making your email address public.

In the beginning, you won't have to worry about being overwhelmed with emails. It will take you some time to build up a large reader base, and it will take your readers some time to write to you. But when they do, be sure to do your best to respond. Even if the message is off topic or seemingly undeserving of a response, your reply will help to establish a bond with that reader. The more personal bonds you forge, the more likely you are to develop relationships with people who frequent your blog. And the more likely they'll continue to come back, and even recommend your blog to others via word of mouth or social media.

Often a Contact page will grow over time. Some of the most successful blogs include different ways of getting in touch, depending on who's making the contact. For example, you may have one email address that you use for potential advertisers, one that you use for general inquiries from readers, and one for people who'd like to write a guest post for your blog.

Giving details on how people can get in touch with you, and what they should expect in return, is a good way to avoid email overload once your blog reaches a larger audience.

RESOURCES PAGE

The Resources page (or Links) is a page on your blog where you can direct your readers to additional content in the field outside of your blog posts. This page of links may include papers or articles written by you or other established experts in your niche. It may include a reading list, with links to books on the same topic on *Amazon.com*. It may include the very sources that you use when writing your posts.

Often, bloggers will include a list of other blogs and bloggers in the same niche that they wish to recommend to their users.

This is often referred to as a *blogroll*. A blogroll is a list of trusted bloggers in the area that you may have a working relationship with. A blogroll can serve a couple of purposes. In addition to providing resources for your readers, it gives you a way to connect with other bloggers in the space (something that we discuss in more detail in the next section of this book). It gives you something to offer other bloggers, as a link to their blog will be something that most will be very eager to receive—and oftentimes they'll link back to your blog, too.

ADVERTISER PAGE

If you wish to accept advertising on your blog as a way of making money, then an Advertiser page is key. This page promotes the fact that you accept advertising, instead of making potential advertisers guess. Be as direct as you want to be on this page.

Most potential advertisers are looking for a couple of key pieces of information, which you can either choose to provide on this page or hold back until they first contact you.

The first piece of information they're looking for is the type of readers you attract. Often they can tell this just from your content, but if you want to give them some added incentive, then include some simple demographic information. For example, "women in their 30s and 40s that spend X number of dollars each year on travel." This is a cue to advertisers that the readers of your blog are likely to respond to ads from airlines or other vacation booking services.

The second piece of information that advertisers are looking for is the amount of readers you attract. This information can usually be garnered without your providing it from a free service like *Compete.com,* but it doesn't hurt to showcase your numbers here. Boast about your thousands of monthly visitors, your enormous Facebook or Twitter following, or your dedicated subscribers.

Finally, potential advisers want to know what kinds of ads you accept and how much they cost. Here you can show them the sizes and placement of the ads in relation to your content. Usually a banner at the top or along the side of each post will suffice.

Pricing is something that most bloggers won't display publicly, giving them the ability to negotiate fresh with each new advertiser. When you're just starting out, keep your prices low. Give your advertisers an incentive to try you out. This will lead to more money down the road as you can prove the success that comes with advertising on your blog.

I want to quickly diverge here to talk a little bit more about advertising and your brand. Most beginning bloggers fit into one of two camps. Either they're eager to get ads up on their blogs so they can start earning money, or they're against displaying ads of any kind on their blogs because they fear users will find them annoying and won't come back. The truth is, the best practice is to find a middle ground.

When you're just starting out, there's a danger of crowding your blog with ads before you've established a reader base. The revenue will come later, so don't rush into it.

But once you've established yourself and your blog has a loyal readership, ads won't hurt you. Most readers expect to see ads on blogs, and they won't be turned off by simple ads that fit the page. Where ads have the potential to create an annoyance is when they inhibit a reader's ability to consume the content on your blog. This is why popup ads are so hated. Keep your ads above and beside the content, so that readers can continue to enjoy your blog posts as they always have. But don't worry too much about ads on your blog hurting your brand. You'll find that most readers won't care.

SALES PAGE

The Sales page is an additional page on your blog to sell products or services. This isn't a necessity, but many bloggers will be trying to earn money from selling their products or services, and this page will give them an opportunity to do that in an area away from the main content of the blog.

Maybe you're blogging about marketing and advertising and you're hoping to sell your services as a consultant. Maybe you're a fashion designer and you'd like to sell your designs. Maybe you're a writer and you want to increase your book sales.

The Sales page gives you a place to present your value proposition, establish prices, and provide people with a way to either pay and purchase something right from your blog, click on a link to another website like *Amazon.com* where they can make a purchase, or get in touch with you because they're interested in what you're selling.

Many bloggers start out without anything to sell, but once they establish themselves in the field, they find that the best way to make money is by selling products or services from their blog. This page may be something that you add at a later time.

Design Matters

1 Why is blog design so important?

Good visuals and curated design give authority and credibility and affect perceived usability.

A bit of originality allows you to be recognized.

A good design with structured and quality content contribute to keep the users on your website the longest.

2 What mistakes have you seen in blog design?

The most frequent mistakes I see are that designers try to replicate the design and the style of other successful blogs.

There are inherent problems related to this approach.

· Sometimes the original design is not so good.

· Often yours is a different problem that requires a different solution in order to work.

It's much better to try to understand why this solution is used and why it works in that context.

Other frequent blog design mistakes:

· Cluttered interfaces with the attempt to include as much content as possible in a webpage.

· Advertisements placed in misleading ways.

· Designs without a precise personality, in an attempt to please too many people.

3 What are some of your favorite blog designs?

· *rainypixels.com*
A very good one; it combines a minimal design with personality. To say nothing about the content, it's very thoughtful and never banal.

· *ilovetypography.com*
A must-read for type lovers with a great use of negative space and, obviously, with great typography.

· *elliotjaystocks.com/blog*
A very minimal but equally effective approach.

· *sachagreif.com*
A pleasure to browse through.

· *blog.omusicawards.com*
A totally different approach from those listed above. I'm totally in love with this design; it's creative, curated, and so tailored to the audience.

—Michela Chiucini
Web Is Love
webislove.com

THE FINISHED PRODUCT

You've named your blog. You've purchased a URL to host your blog that supports that name.

You've created a logo that showcases a little bit of your style and color scheme.

You've established a look and feel for your blog that utilizes color to welcome readers and help them feel at home on your blog.

You're using a font that makes reading easy.

And you've added some supporting pages to round out your blog and create a fuller user experience.

This is your blog. It's the largest piece of *you* that readers will come to know. It's the very foundation of your brand, which you'll use to grow and find success. In the material that follows, we'll take what you've built and start to look outward. We'll discuss ways that you can grow your brand by reaching out to others, establishing yourself on social media platforms, and earning credibility. And then we'll take it one step further and work through the various ways that you can attract an audience and monetize or earn money with your blog.

WE HOPE YOU'RE ENJOYING THE BOOK SO FAR.

Many of the early successful bloggers started out with little or no formal training. That's because they invented the field, and no training was made available to them. They came before us and paved the way. And through them, we've learned what it takes to make it as a blogger.

At the New York Institute of Career Development, we put those techniques into our Complete Course in Professional Blogging. Not only that, but we rounded up hundreds of successful bloggers who were eager to share their input and advice with people who were learning the field.

Our students are new bloggers, experienced bloggers who want to improve the quality of their content and drive more traffic, and bloggers who have been at it for awhile and want to use their blog to earn real money. Many dream of the day when they can blog full time, earning as much money as they would with a full-time job.

IT'S A LONG JOURNEY, BUT WE'RE HERE TO HELP MAKE SURE YOU GET THERE.

We invite you to take a look at our course risk-free and decide if it's right for you. Our no-risk refund policy promises that you have 21 days after you receive your first set of materials to review them and decide whether our course is right for you. If not, you can return it and we'll refund every penny. If we were not extremely confident in the quality of our course, we could not afford to offer such a strong refund policy.

REQUEST A FREE COURSE CATALOG AND RECEIVE A TUITION DISCOUNT CERTIFICATE

WWW.NYICD.COM/BOOK

NY|CD

"WITH OVER 50,000 NEW BLOGS STARTING EACH DAY, BLOGGERS WHO TAKE THIS COURSE WILL HAVE MAJOR ADVANTAGES OVER EVERYONE ELSE IN THIS CROWDED FIELD. THEY'LL BE MORE PREPARED TO STAY WITH THEIR BLOG, GROW THEIR AUDIENCE, SHARPEN THEIR BRAND, THINK MORE STRATEGICALLY, IMPROVE THEIR WRITING AND CORE BLOGGING SKILLS, AND MAKE MORE MONEY ONLINE."

- JAY JOHNSON, CREATOR OF THE PROFESSIONAL BLOGGING COURSE
AND SUCCESSFUL BLOGGER AT DESIGN2SHARE.COM

REQUEST A FREE COURSE CATALOG AND RECEIVE A TUITION DISCOUNT CERTIFICATE
1.800.445.7279

GROWING YOUR BRAND

Defining your brand is the hard part.
Now that you've taken care of business on that front, you can move on to the fun stuff.

Think of yourself as a small business. You now know who you are and what you want to say to the world. But is anyone listening? Not yet.

This next section is Marketing 101. Now that you've defined your brand, you need to share it with the world and establish yourself and your blog in the space.

You need to grab your megaphone and shout out to the world, "Here I am!"

In the sections that follow, we'll show you a number of ways that you can grow your brand. There are online tools and channels for you to take advantage of. And we'll provide tried-and-true strategies for establishing yourself in your marketplace. From writing articles and guest posts, to networking with other bloggers in the space, to using social media to connect, share, and spread the word, you'll learn what it takes to take a good brand and use it to gain awareness.

This is a key step in the branding process. The tips and techniques you'll learn here will build what we call in the marketing industry "brand awareness." Once people know about you, you can start to "sell" to them.

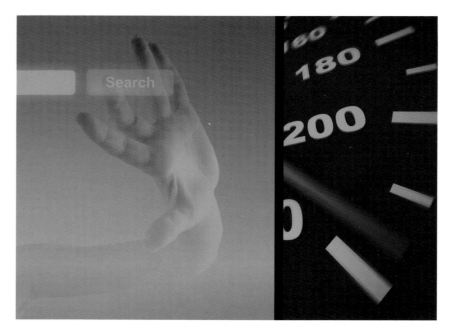

SEO: A BRIEF INTRODUCTION

If ever you needed a background on *search engine optimization* (SEO), it's right now. Why? Because in the sections that follow, I'll continue to refer back to SEO as if you already know what it is and why it's important. And I can't make that assumption unless I put it right here in the text for all to see.

If you already have a basic understanding of SEO and how it will affect your blog, I still suggest that you read this part of the book, as the explanation that I provide might be a bit different from anything you've heard before, and will relate directly to the advice that follows. I've made every attempt to keep this as concise and interesting as possible. (I apologize in advance if you feel that I've failed on either front!)

Search engines crawl their way around the Web creating updated databases of content. When you type one or more words into a search box, the engine's internal algorithms return ranked lists of links to sites that match the search terms, prompting the results pages that we're all very familiar with.

The aim of SEO is to try to get your blog near the top of those search results for keywords and phrases related to your blog or brand.

Content and links are crucial to how high up on the search engine rankings your site will be. Your goal is to have your site show up in the first two pages of search results (the higher up, the better), as most searchers won't go much deeper into the millions of links that are returned by any given search.

So the question is: How can you get your blog to rank higher in any given search and steer more traffic your way?

KEYWORDS ARE KEY

Your blog will be filled with words, which is a great start. The words that you use most often in your blog posts and in the rest of the content on your blog will be recognized by Google and other search engines. So it's important to remember to use the keywords that are most relevant and unique to your blog as often as possible. This way, search engines know what your blog is about, and will direct searches on that topic your way.

High-quality written content is the single most fundamental element of effective search engine optimization. Search engine crawlers can only "read" words. They can't "look at" pictures or video or product logos. They can't "listen" to a podcast and understand it. It's all about the written word.

Keywords are the words and phrases searchers use, not necessarily the ones you use when you're talking with friends or colleagues. A doctor wouldn't

hesitate to say "myocardial infarction." The average searcher is more likely to look for "heart attack." A Corvette enthusiast wouldn't think twice about her enthusiasm for a "383 Stroker 450 HP." But the average searcher is more likely to look for a "Corvette engine."

How do you find out what popular keywords are in your field?

Brainstorm a list of the words and phrases a searcher might use to find your blog. The trick with keywords is to be specific.

The first thing you want to do is to forget broad terms. If you have a blog on photography, the broader terms like "photography" or "photographer" are less likely to bring you traffic than more specific terms like "Alexandria wedding photographer" or "portrait photographer in Indiana" or "Cascade Mountain skiing photos."

Ask non-bloggers such as friends, family, clients, or colleagues what terms come to mind.

Take this list of terms and run it through Google's keyword tool, found at *adwords.google.com/select /KeywordToolExternal*.

The best keywords are relevant to your site, have higher than average traffic, and lower than average competition.

This information should narrow down your list of keywords and give you a better idea of what terms to use in your posts in order to bring in the most traffic. Since search engines are the most prominent source of traffic for most websites, this is a key step in building a successful blog.

WRITING SEO-FRIENDLY COPY

Use keywords wisely in your text, but also with a degree of moderation.

In SEO, the term *keyword density* refers to the percentage of times a keyword or phrase appears on a page compared to the total number of words on that page. If the keywords you've settled on appear too often, search engine spiders may assume you're *keyword stuffing,* or abusing the use of keywords.

The search engine's algorithms can actually reduce that page's ranking for the relevant keyword(s) because the page looks "spammy" and artificial to human visitors.

LINKS

The second most important part of your search engine optimization strategy: links. Links to your blog, links from within your own content, links to other pages on your site, social media site links, or links to and from other websites and blogs are vital to improving your SEO, attracting new visitors, and building a successful blog.

Google and other search engines realize that you can stuff your blog full of keywords, but the blog still might be worthless. How do they rectify this? By looking at links. Google uses links to your page or posts as a kind of proof of credibility. When someone links to one of your posts, they're telling people that this is something worth checking out. And Google takes that to mean that your site is more credible than if no one else linked to it.

Some of the tips that follow will address the specific goal of increasing the number of links you have coming into your blog—"external" links. Linking from one post to another, from posts to other pages on your site, and from other pages on your site back to individual posts are all ways you can add "internal" links that will also help to address this goal. In general, the more links you have to your blog, the better. And when these links come from reputable sites like newspapers, popular blogs, or educational (.edu) domains, it's even better.

NETWORK WITH OTHER BLOGGERS

When you start your blog, you're not doing it in a vacuum. Rather, you're becoming part of the blogosphere. The blogosphere is the great, unwieldy, confounding thing that includes blogs on everything from funny cat photos to political ranting. It includes you and every other blog and blogger out there. It's a community of people using blogging as a creative outlet, money-making enterprise, news distributor, or coping mechanism.

Networking with your fellow bloggers is critical to making your own brand succeed.

While you want to have your own brand stand out from the pack, you also need to connect with the rest of the pack. Developing symbiotic relationships with fellow bloggers is a crucial step in this process.

Networking involves interacting with other bloggers through a variety of different channels. These channels can be as simple as commenting on other people's blogs, or responding to comments by bloggers left on your own site. Another option is to reach out to like-minded bloggers about topics of interest, or to join a number of blog forums that circulate ideas about a certain topic.

To give your blog further depth and exposure, you should create accounts on all the major social media platforms such as Facebook, Twitter, Google+, etc. (more on these later) and update them frequently. This will give your audience increased access to your brand, growing your following exponentially while simultaneously making it easier for bloggers to find you.

Social media networking will also allow you to share content instantly with other bloggers and link back to your own blog to create a feedback loop that drives traffic.

"The Andrews" at Movable Media, Boer and Eisner, are quick to point out how the expansion of social media has led to networking and marketing becoming further intertwined, opening up additional avenues for the modern blogger. "At the same time, the growth of the Internet economy has also created new ways for marketers to reach their target audiences. BI (Before Internet), marketers reached their prospects virtually exclusively via so-called outbound channels: advertising, collateral, direct mail, etc. AI (After Internet), marketers created websites so that their prospects could seek them out and educate themselves. And the advent and continuing growth of

social channels—Twitter, Facebook and Google+ chief among them, but with many more like Pinterest, StumbleUpon, and others growing in importance and reach every day—has increased the complexity facing marketers."

In addition to striving to become a go-to source within a specific niche, it's extremely beneficial to establish yourself as a middleman for neighboring niches. This means that you're constantly helping your fellow bloggers out, either by volunteering your knowledge to help them achieve their goals (which will lead them to link back to you), or by connecting them with someone who can. Thus more bloggers will trust you and turn to you with opportunities, and your network will expand in turn.

Other networking methods include directory additions, joining online mailing lists, utilizing RSS feeds, and creating a concise elevator pitch to summarize what you do and what service your blog offers. All of these strategies remind us that successful bloggers work to establish their brand in a number of different avenues, and the work of creating a successful online brand involves more than just working on your own site. The external channels that allow you to connect with other bloggers and like-minded people in your field are just as important as the work you do creating great content. These are the tools at your disposal to get your content out to the world.

GUEST POSTS

One way of connecting with other blogs is by making "guest posts," in which you write a post for another blog. The host blog then provides a link back to your blog, bringing you more readers.

"The value proposition behind the traditional guest blog post is a simple one," says Andrew Eisner. "You (the publisher) have an audience, and I (the guest blogger) have some relevant content. Let's fuse these things together: I'll give you the content, and in return, can you give me some exposure and maybe some backlinks?"

As a blogger, you should understand the inherent value of guest posting for both parties before offering your services to other blogs.

The guest post is one strategy that bloggers use to gain links to their blog. A *backlink,* so called because it's a link back to your blog, isn't only important because of the readers it will send directly to your blog. It will also help your overall SEO, as we alluded to earlier.

Pamela Wilson stresses the importance of using guest posting both as a networking tool and as a vehicle for self-promotion. "Once you've established yourself, go out to other bloggers and offer to guest post to help spread your message. Direct people back to your site, where you can give them something to sign up for or other content to look through," she says.

You can start by seeking out blogs that are similar to your own, and, first of all, becoming a follower. Next, read the blog you're going to approach, and read it every time a new post is made so that you're familiar not only with the content but also with the flow. You don't want to write a guest post repeating something the host just posted, but it would work to write a post that offers a new angle on something the host just posted. Finally, approach the host: send an email with a couple of sentences describing what your guest post will be and how you think it will contribute to their blog.

Often, popular blogs receive the most requests for a guest post because exposure on their site is better than exposure on a blog with only a few readers. Because of this, those blogs often have specific policies on accepting guest posts available on their blog. Make sure to look for these instructions before reaching out to a blogger for the first time. If you don't follow the guidelines that they provide, you won't be making a great first impression.

The Andrews at Movable Media know from experience that it's imperative to strike a balance between "give" and "take" in order for both sides (the host and the guest) to get the most out of a given guest post. "To maximize the value of a guest blog, ideally both parties would have shared access to analytics and share incentives, responsibilities, and rewards for promoting the content to an audience. The right approach really works—at Movable Media we saw as much as a 500% lift in traffic per article for one client once we moved from providing 'content' to providing 'Content with an Audience,' by using authors with audiences, and giving them the tools and incentives to activate them. But there's no reason why this approach should be exclusive to content marketing: it can and should be applied to all guest blog posts, even those grass-roots intra-blog barter transactions."

Frequent guest posting is a great way to build a following and to establish yourself as a trustworthy resource in a given niche, both key factors for a growing brand. But don't be afraid of getting rejected. Be persistent.

Guest posting is a numbers game, meaning that the more bloggers you reach out to, the more exposure you'll be able to get for your blog.

ARTICLE WRITING

Writing articles and getting them published in online publications is a more traditional way of bringing in readers and promoting your brand. But just because it's more traditional doesn't mean it's not worth doing. This is a strategy that many brands and bloggers alike have used to bring in new audiences and improve SEO.

Say you have a blog on vintage cars; an article you write on the charms of the '67 Mustang that appears in *Vintage Cars Magazine* will link back to you, and will help confirm your status as an expert. The loyal readers of the magazine will view your inclusion as a certification that you're a credible source in that particular content area. They'll then likely read your article and, based on the quality of the content, judge whether or not to continue on to your blog for additional insight. In this scenario, the content is driven by the subject matter of the magazine, and your hope is to garner popularity in addition to the money you'll be paid for having your article published.

But how can you expect a reputable magazine or online publication to publish something you write? The short answer is, you can't. But that's not the only option available to you. A quick Google search for "article submission sites" returns a slew of sites, and lists of sites that accept articles submitted by you or anyone else with some expertise on a given topic. Some of these sites require you to sign up before posting. This is recommended. Posting articles that offer quality content and link back to your blog is another way of growing your reach and improving SEO.

For a list of the top article submission sites, check out *vretoolbar.com /articles/directories.php*.

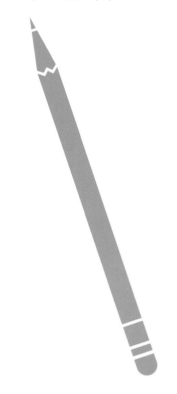

SOCIAL MEDIA

The importance of social media when it comes to branding can't be overstated. The ever-growing popularity and widespread use of social media should be reason enough for you to think hard about your brand before your blog goes live and you start blogging regularly. Once your blog is up and running, you won't be able to go online without, directly or indirectly, representing your blog. As we told you at the beginning of this book, you are a brand. And you're representing that brand at all times.

This means that if you're really an acerbic wag and your friends expect sarcastic humor when they see you posting on Facebook, you should think twice before starting a blog with a brand that'll be associated with calming yoga poses. While many people attempt to keep their social media usage separate from their "professional" lives, this can create confusion and sometimes result in inadvertent spillover that can hurt your brand.

So before you start blogging, it's important to develop a social media strategy or game plan.

This strategy is something that you can stick to, developed to help you network with other bloggers, interact with fans and readers, and promote your content to a wider audience. Since social media offers all different types of interactions, it's a no-brainer when it comes to promoting your blog. Without it, you'll have a much harder time trying to achieve success.

"Social distribution is increasingly critical for content," says Andrew Boer. "No matter the topic, social media allows individual content creators and curators to put ideas directly in front of interested and engaged people. Those audiences can in turn create communities around the ideas and influences with which they identify."

In the marketing world, many of the largest companies are still learning just how valuable social media can be. They're exploring with new ways of connecting with consumers. And to be perfectly honest, they're taking advantage of techniques developed and perfected by bloggers. So I've tried to assemble a quick starter kit for you here, made up of descriptions of the major networks and how you can use them, and some time-tested methods of establishing yourself on the various networks.

"Using social media to build relationships shows how active, responsive, and engaged you are and therefore brings people back to your site," Ros Gardner says. "Besides, chatting with friends on Facebook is a lot more fun than doing paid advertising and is a lot less expensive, too!"

FACEBOOK

The world's largest social network, with over 800 million users worldwide, Facebook is a popular network for bloggers for a couple of reasons. First, because of its size and popularity, it's a logical place to start getting involved in social media. And second, because everything you do on Facebook encourages sharing, it's a great place to share content and grow your audience.

On Facebook, you're able to use your own personal page, or you can create a brand page specific to your business. People will have the ability to "Like" or subscribe to your page, meaning they'll see updates from you every time you post something to your Facebook page.

Facebook is a great place to share blog posts, photos, videos, and announcements. Doing this puts your content in front of a new audience, and encourages commenting and sharing of that content.

You can direct people to "Like" your blog on Facebook simply by adding the "Like" button to your website. That way people who have a Facebook account already can connect with you in a very familiar way.

If people start talking about you on Facebook, you've already made progress.

TWITTER

Made popular by the variety of celebrities who use it, its ability to break the news before major networks, and the uniquely short length of its messages (known as "Tweets"), Twitter continues to rise as the number two social network in the world. And where Facebook tends to be a bit lengthy and confusing, Twitter's simplicity makes it a popular choice among anyone wishing to join the online conversation.

For bloggers, Twitter is a common choice because it allows you to publish your own content as well as other content you find interesting, and to do so quickly and easily. You can follow other people in your field to receive updates from them, send messages directly to others, and keep your followers up to date on your business.

Just like Facebook, it's common to place a Twitter icon on your blog posts so that people can quickly add you to the list of people they follow without having to leave your site.

If you have a unique voice and can keep things interesting, Twitter is a great place to attract a crowd.

LINKEDIN

Born as the social network for "professionals," LinkedIn aims to differentiate itself from Facebook and Twitter by making things "more serious." Popular now among job hunters, serial networkers, and companies wanting to fill vacancies, this network offers some advantages Twitter and Facebook don't.

As a blogger, building your LinkedIn profile should revolve around experience and credibility, networking, and future business opportunities. Depending on your field and area of expertise, usage will be different. But LinkedIn is a great place to connect with other experts in the field and share information with them.

GOOGLE+

Google Plus is Google's answer to social media. Building off of popular services like search and Gmail, they've created an all-inclusive profile for every Web user, should you choose to join. Still relatively new, Google+ hasn't achieved the kind of growth and adoption that the other networks have. However, because it's operated by a company with as powerful a Web presence as Google, it should be on your radar.

For bloggers, creating an account and sharing your posts is a good way to get started.

PINTEREST

Pinterest is a new network that has grown in popularity over the last year or two. Using images, users create a scrapbook of articles, pages, videos, and pictures by "pinning" them and assigning them to boards that can be made public or private. The network is popular in areas that are more visual and creative, such as fashion, photography, and crafts.

For bloggers, allowing your readers to "Pin" your posts by adding the Pin It button to your site is a good way to get started and gain exposure through this network.

YOUTUBE

You should always consider adding video and other dynamic media to your blog (more on this later in the book). And if you have video to share, YouTube is where you should host it. The most popular video sharing site, YouTube accounts for a huge percentage of online video consumption. It's free to use and anyone can upload and share content.

For bloggers, creating a YouTube channel for your blog is a great way to share your content with people who are already looking for video content. Use it to drive traffic to your blog, and embed videos back on your blog for people to view as they read through your posts. You'll notice that the most popular blogs are using more and more video, because it attracts a larger audience than text alone.

YOUR SOCIAL ROADMAP

When you're just starting out, social media can seem a bit daunting. I just listed six different networks, and I didn't even begin to scratch the surface. But don't fret. You don't have to use them all, and you'll get more comfortable using them over time.

I recommend at least Facebook and Twitter to start, and you can expand into the others at a later time. For Facebook, you should create a page for your brand that is separate from your personal account, which makes sharing and interacting with people more seamless and less confusing. The page will reinforce your brand, and it will become an additional outlet for your content.

For details on how to do this, visit *facebook.com/pages/create.php.*

On Twitter, create an account and begin following people in your field. You can share your posts with a link and headline, find other content in your field to share, and send messages back and forth between other bloggers and your readers.

For details on how to do this, visit the Twitter Help Center at *support.twitter .com/articles/100990-how-to-sign-up -on-twitter.*

Start Small

How did you learn to successfully blog and build your business?

From building my first Web page, to making money online and building out all of my blogs ... it was all self-taught with endless hours of work and a desire to learn and do better.

There are plenty of free sources and videos online to help you along the way, but you need to actually get started and learn through your actions, success, and failures.

—Zac Johnson
ZacJohnson.com
zacjohnson.com

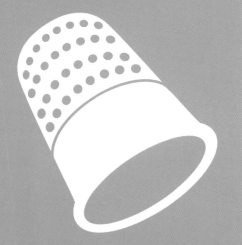

Once you've established yourself in these two large networks, the others won't seem quite so scary.

You'll learn shortcuts to keep the time you devote to social media limited while still getting a lot out of it. And you'll establish relationships with people online that will help your brand grow and succeed.

Andrew Boer and Andrew Eisner are quick to point out just how powerful a promotional tool social media has become for the aspiring writer/blogger. "One of the most positive recent developments is that writers of all stripes now have the tools to develop and maintain their own following, their own independent 'circulation'—through Facebook, Twitter, their blogs, and across the Web.

"Many of the key traditional functions of the publisher are now handled directly by the writer. Writers can not only reach an audience, but can measure it, monetize it, and even bring it with them through links, updates, and tweets."

Social media has brought the blogger and target audience closer than ever before, allowing your brand the opportunity to be experienced on a larger scale with greater immediacy. Take advantage of it!

CREDIBILITY AND BRANDING

Before we close this chapter, it's important to reflect back on what you've read. You've learned a number of ways to establish and grow your brand outside of your own blog. You've learned how to generate links to your content, create relationships with other bloggers, and gain new readers.

But in all of this, what should not get lost is the importance of establishing credibility. So much of what you're trying to do with your blog when you're just starting out has to do with becoming credible. Bloggers who aren't seen as credible sources of information in their field will never achieve success. And you establish credibility by making connections, proving your expertise, and getting others to provide proof of your credibility through links and recommendations.

You're well aware that you know what you're talking about on your blog. The problem is, potential readers don't know that. And few will trust you without some sort of "proof." Getting involved in the blogosphere and in social media are the ways you can help to establish trust in the digital space. This will make attracting audiences, and earning money using the strategies provided in the third and final chapter of this book, that much easier.

USING YOUR BRAND

You've come a long way.
Now it's time to put what you've learned to good use.

You've learned how to define who you are and what your blog is all about, how to use other online media to help establish yourself in the minds of readers and consumers, and how to generate brand awareness. It's been like giving you a whole marketing class.

But this chapter is what most bloggers picked this book up for. Now we get to learn how to use your newly established brand to grow your online audience and maximize your income.

Like we said way back in the beginning of this book, different bloggers will have different goals. Success means different things to different people. But if you're interested in more readers to sell ads, sell products, sell services, or raise money and awareness for your cause, a good brand will make a big difference.

In the sections that follow, you'll learn exactly where your brand fits into your overall marketing plan. You'll learn how to plan and add new revenue producing activities to your blog. And you'll learn how to continue to refine and monitor your brand in order to keep up with changing trends, new competitors, and reader habits.

Most bloggers struggle to earn money.

Earning money online isn't as easy as many people would like to think it is. The fact that you've come this far means that you have what it takes, and you're willing to put in the effort needed to succeed. Use that fact as motivation going forward and you can join the elite bloggers that are already out there earning real money.

DRIVING TRAFFIC

Without customers, a company can't expect to make money. So they spend a little time and energy building a great brand that attracts lots of customers, give them something to buy, and then follow through to make sure that they're satisfied customers who continue to shop with them and refer their friends.

For bloggers, the same dynamic is at play. We spent the bulk of this book talking about how to build and grow a strong brand so that you can take the next step and earn money with your blog. But there's a very important step in between that needs to be addressed first: driving traffic, or visitors, to your blog.

Without visitors, there's no money to be made. Every monetization scheme in this chapter relies on driving visitors to your blog. Once you have visitors, you can sell ads or you can sell products or you can generate business. Without them, you don't have a successful blog.

And for bloggers, visitors mean more than just someone who lands on your blog. Yes, that's the first challenge. But what we really want are readers, *engaged* readers. Let's go over a few ways of driving visitors to your blog and then talk about how we can keep them there and turn casual visitors into engaged readers.

WHERE THEY COME FROM

Where do your visitors come from? If you're like most blogs or other websites, a large majority of your visitors will come from either search engines or social media. These are the two most important drivers of traffic, which is why we devoted rather large sections earlier in this book to them.

People are going to find you, but they're going to start somewhere else.

They're going to be searching for information similar to what you provide on Google or Bing, or they're going to be more casually surfing the Web or their favorite social network and stumble upon something that leads them your way. This is why staying active in social media and working on good search engine optimization strategies are so important. They're the traffic drivers. They're how you get discovered.

All of the other ways we discussed for you to grow your brand are also potential traffic drivers. Writing guest posts and articles will get you visitors who are reading your content on another site. Any paid advertising you do or offline attention that you or your brand gets will help send people your way.

But it all starts with good content. When you provide quality content on your blog, you're laying the foundation upon which everything else is built. Remember, much of the SEO work we talked about in the previous chapter starts with the content on your site, the keywords you use in your posts, and the headlines you use. And without good content, the networking you do in social media won't do much for you.

When someone lands on your site for the first time, it's like someone walking into a store or a restaurant for the first time. It's your chance to make a good first impression. You do that with your brand, and you do that with great blog posts that really engage the reader.

RETURN VISITORS

Getting people to your site for the first time is a big step, but that's not where the challenge ends. A visitor is measured and counted when he or she lands on a page of your site. And growing that total number is certainly one of the goals. But the real key to creating a successful blog is turning those visitors into return visitors or subscribers.

Return visitors, as the name suggests, are people who come back to your blog more than once.

Those people liked what they saw so much the first time that they come back looking for more content, whether to read a new post or view your About page to learn more about you. They're the equivalent of loyal customers to a company. They're fans of your brand. And gaining more of them will lead to a successful blog.

Your blog may not get return visitors as much as it gets subscribers. In the blogosphere, people have become comfortable "subscribing" to blogs that they want to continue to read instead of returning to the site each time they want to find a new post. Subscribing makes it simple, because you only get the new posts, and you get them right when they're first published.

Having an option for readers to subscribe via RSS, real simple syndication, is key to growing your reader base. This is how most people who read blogs do it. They'll use an RSS reader of some sort, like Google Reader, and use it to follow a number of blogs that they're interested in.

You can also offer the opportunity for people to subscribe via email, using a service like Feedburner. Some people prefer to get emails from a few blogs that they follow instead of using an RSS reader. And others will instead choose to follow you on Facebook or Twitter if they know they can receive new content that way.

Any way they do it, your biggest fans will be your subscribers.

And as that number goes up, so too does your ability to use your blog to earn money.

Come Back for More

I've seen steady readership and subscription growth over the past years in my home design blog. I've used these sneaky features to help me acquire steady, loyal readers.

Sometimes I post longer-form articles and show an excerpt that requires readers to click to read the second part of the text and photos. This adds more page views to my site stats and it starts to get readers in the habit of clicking around in the rest of my site; that first click warms them up!

I make it easy for first-time readers to become subscribers by adding this link to my RSS feed at the end of each and every post: Click here to subscribe to our daily design videos and features.

The best advice I ever got was to increase my posts from three times a week to five times a week. (I'd blog every day of the week, but I need to rest on the weekends!) More content on a blog, delivered with extreme regularity, attracts more traffic. Seriously, you shouldn't expect readers to get very excited about your blog if you're only creating one post a week. Blog readers have big content appetites.

—Jay Johnson
Design2Share
design2share.com

PASSIVE VERSUS ACTIVE READERS

Not all readers are created alike. And your content can have a lot to do with how readers interact with your blog.

A passive reader, for the purposes of this book, is someone who casually reads your blog. They may only come once, they may return more than once, and they may even subscribe. These are all good things, but there's another step that you want readers to take. You want them to interact with your blog in some way other than just reading.

This "action" is what makes someone an active reader. Active readers are great!

Active readers are people who leave comments, start conversations, share your posts in social media, refer their friends to your blog, and contact you with questions or feedback. They're a blog's version of early adopters and brand ambassadors. They'll be the first to offer feedback, and they'll get conversations going around your brand that will pique the interest of others.

The more active readers you have, the more likely you are to be successful. But active readers don't just show up one day and start making noise. There are ways that you can (and should) elicit this type of interaction on your blog. Here are a few.

ASK QUESTIONS

If you use your posts only to state facts or opinions, that sounds to your readers like you're speaking *at* them. You're not asking for feedback, and so they're not likely to provide any. Asking questions on your blog and in your social media feeds for people to answer is a way of getting them involved.

When people feel like their feedback is desired, and that what they have to say matters, they're more likely to get involved.

OPEN-ENDED POSTS

Similar to asking questions, leaving some of your posts open-ended will encourage people to chime in with their own thoughts. If you state your opinion on a given subject, end the post by stating that you'd like to know whether or not people agree with you. This way, readers know that you're looking for information from them to advance the conversation, and they'll be happy to provide it if they have an opinion on the subject.

ASK FOR COMMENTS

Just like your open-ended posts, asking for comments at the end of each post will help get a conversation started around your content. But don't just ask for comments and leave it at that. Make sure you follow along and get involved in the comments section yourself. Create that two-way street of communication that makes your readers feel like welcome and valued members of a community that centers around your brand.

SURVEYS AND POLLS

Surveys and polls are easy ways to get people involved in your posts. By asking for their input, you're getting them to take an action that goes beyond just reading. Surveys and polls can be on anything related to your field, and can even be surveys about the type of content you're providing.

Some of the most successful bloggers regularly ask their readers the equivalent of "How's my driving?" You may get some criticisms, but that's a good thing. Your readers will become the best focus group you could ever ask for, and they'll help you steer your brand in the right direction (more on this later).

GIVEAWAYS

Using contests, sweepstakes, and giveaways on your blog is a great way to elicit action from your readers. People love free stuff, and the readers of your blog are no different. You can offer one lucky winner a free hat, shirt, book, etc. just for sharing your post on Twitter, or for leaving a comment, or for subscribing to your RSS feed.

Often, people are more than willing to do what it is you want them to do, whether that's sharing your content with others, subscribing, or commenting on your blog. The biggest hurdles are just making it easy for them to do so and providing the smallest of incentives. Even if giving something away for free isn't an option, great content can serve as a top-notch incentive in and of itself.

This way, you get people excited, and you provide them with an incentive to do something you want them to do.

ONGOING EVALUATION

As you continue to blog, you need to find ways to continuously monitor your brand. This way, you'll be able to make changes to the brand when needed, refining it and improving upon it as you go.

Zac Johnson points out the importance of staying ahead of the game, emphasizing the need to always keep thinking about tomorrow. "Since blogging can be one of the slower methods for creating a business or revenue source online, it's important to always think about the future of your blog and its branding at all times. When going live with your first blog, you'll want to make sure that you have a brandable name and logo that will help identify you in the crowd and allow people to recognize and remember your brand as an authority for information within your niche," he says.

"As your blog continues to grow over the years with more content and readers, your brand will also continue to grow."

Companies call this *brand management*, and when things get really bad, *rebranding*. They take what they've already created, and start fresh. They spend millions of dollars to change their logo, or run television ads promoting themselves in a new way. At the end of the day, they want consumers to see them differently. Sometimes it works, and sometimes it's too little, too late.

For new bloggers, it's not as much rebranding as it is brand upkeep and brand growth. Things change over time. Fads come and go, the economy goes up and down, and readers will come and go.

But the core brand that you've built using the tips in this book won't change all that much.

It will just need to be revisited from time to time so that you can make sure everything is in working order, and you're still achieving the goals you set out when you created the brand.

Just as you wouldn't send your kid off to first grade and not check his homework until college, you also won't just send your blog into the blogosphere and assume it's working at optimal capacity every day. "Encouraging feedback by allowing readers to post comments and send personal messages through a contact form on your blog are the two most effective ways to monitor and control your brand," Ros Gardner says.

When you hear feedback that's less than positive, don't just get mad and turn away—instead, listen. "Any negative feedback about problems with your product must be dealt with and corrected swiftly," Gardner says. "Positive feedback, on the other hand, can be used to build out a testimonials section on your blog."

We talked about the importance of listening to your readers in order to learn what they like, what they don't like, and what they want more of. As you continue to blog and your readership continues to grow, catering to the early readers who participated in your blog in some way is essential. They'll steer you toward success, and they'll bring you more readers as time goes on.

An essential part of the ongoing evaluation of your brand should be to listen to this group of people, and to continue to elicit feedback from them so that you know how you're doing. I've seen many blogs grow quickly, only to become stale or become boring over time because the bloggers stopped listening to their readers. They had so much early success that they thought they knew all the answers, and they stopped trying, took it easy, and stagnated.

Here's a blogging truism: successful blogging is a marathon, not a sprint. When things are going well, they can always turn sour. Just like when things are going slow, they can always pick up. The most successful bloggers never stop working to better their brand.

In addition to listening to what your readers have to say, you can keep abreast of what's happening with your blog by setting up a Google Alert so you'll know every time it's mentioned. Google Alerts are email updates of the latest relevant Google results (Web, news, etc.) based on a set of keywords or phrases. You can set them up easily by going to *google.com/alerts*.

Try adding alerts for the name of your blog, your name (if that's different), and any other keywords that you'd like to keep an eye on. You can set them to come in once a day, or more or less frequently depending on how often you feel like receiving the emails. These alerts will tell you when Google picks up your content. They might notify you if another blogger or article mentions you, or show you if your posts are picked up or posted somewhere else on the Web. You can visit each link straight from the email, and if there's a mention of you or your brand on another site, you can leave a comment or get in touch with the writer. This is a great way to monitor the conversation around your brand, and to network with others who have found your content useful.

Finally, you can use your blog stats to make sure things are going in the right direction at all times. Most blogging platforms will offer their own stats and analytics so that you can see the basics, such as number of visitors, where they're coming from, and what they're reading. But if that's not enough, you can use a free tool, such as Google Analytics, to get a more in-depth look into the traffic on your blog. Setting it up is easy; begin by registering at *google.com/analytics,* and then adding a small snippet of code they provide to your blog.

By monitoring your blog's traffic, you can learn what posts are the most popular, whether or not you're driving more visitors each month, and where those people are coming from.

This will help you decide if the strategies you're using to grow your blog are working, or if you need to rethink them.

MAKING MONEY

Finally! We've come to the good part. You've put in all the work. You've established and grown a solid brand. You're attracting readers and keeping them interested in what you have to say with great content. It's time to make money using your blog.

Most people think of making money online as selling ads. And while we'll cover advertising as one key way of making money on your blog, there are many other ways that you should consider as well. Often people give up after they try to sell ads and it doesn't work. So I'm going to start with everything else, and get back to ads later.

WRITER FOR HIRE

Good blogging often means good writing. Blogging will give you ample practice to exercise your writing muscles. Look at a blog as a showcase of your writing style and talents. If you're so inclined, put out feelers to blog networks and news sites for guest blogging gigs and, eventually, a paid blogging opportunity. Look for organizations with websites in your content vertical—which you should know about for your blog, regardless—and reach out to those without blogs, offering your assistance. Other opportunities to write for a living may be offline, writing for a local newspaper or magazine, for instance.

CONSULTING SERVICES

If you have a home staging blog, then you have a platform to sell your services as a home stager. Real estate blogs for Realtors, health and fitness blogs for home trainers and masseuses, astrology blogs for astrologers, cooking blogs for caterers, business marketing blogs for business consultants—all of these are examples of how a blog advertises that your services are for hire.

Be sure to include information about what you do and how you work with the public or business sectors in your blog's About page. One blogger we know actually has a "Hire Me!" tab in her navigation bar, and she spells out how she wants to work with her readers.

Your blog should provide potential customers with deep insight into your personality, your points of view, and your depth of knowledge about your content vertical.

PUBLISH A BOOK

We encourage you to explore self-publishing your own print and e-books, but a number of bloggers have landed their own book deals with commercial publishers. Traditional houses will market, advertise, and sell your brand and your blog on their own dime—and that's a great way to expand your brand's influence, reach out to new markets, and increase your blog's traffic. Many bloggers have been able to compile "best of my blog" posts or other content to create their books—but you're a writer at heart, and even coming up with new material on your subject shouldn't be too difficult!

SELL E-BOOKS

Instead of bothering with physical, printed books, as long as your users are online, you might want to offer them e-books for sale. The same rules apply for self-published paperback and hardcover books, except that everything is now electronic. Write your text out in a Word document and convert it to a PDF. Take the PDF to a company that specializes in e-book services like eBookIt!, eBookTemplate-Source.com, Smashwords, or Scribd.

WEBINARS

Webinars are great ways to authoritatively reach your audience and monetize their enthusiasm for your expertise and advice.

A webinar is an online conference, with one person—you, the expert blogger!—lecturing and conducting a question-and-answer session with many people.

Bloggers sign up to use an online webinar service that allows your audience to plan ahead and participate in either a free or paid event. Some webinars allow you to show live video of you talking alongside a PowerPoint presentation of your discussion. Participants log in to the webinar site using a Web address, user name, and password that you provide, and they can either listen to the audio through their computer or phone in.

There are many webinar services you can explore for hosting your online presentations. Most are free if you have under a certain number of participants, with a fee for expanding your audience when your webinars begin to generate buzz with your blogging audience. Free services, perfect for bloggers, include Vyew, Yugma, and Yuuguu.

APPS

Consider developing an app for the iPhone and Droid around your blog. It's a great way to market your brand while making money. Do you have a yoga blog? Develop a "Two-Minute Pose of the Day" app. Is your blog about the Rubik's Cube? Why not a Rubik's Cube app? Apple provides free app development software on its products and site. Actual app-making development just takes time and patience, and an app form to be submitted to Apple or Google.

AFFILIATE MARKETING

One way to make money as a blogger is to participate in one or more affiliate programs. An affiliate program is an online system for marketing products that involves three parties. In essence, you help other people market their products, and you make money every time someone buys through your link.

One of the largest and often one of the more prosperous affiliate marketing programs for bloggers is offered by Amazon. Becoming an Amazon Affiliate is free and simple, and it allows you to "sell" any product offered on Amazon for a small commission.

While Amazon might have everything under the sun for bloggers, there are plenty of other affiliate networks to check out. One or more may be a perfect fit for you and your audience. You can try Click Bank, Share a Sale, and Commission Junction to start.

ADVERTISING

As mentioned before, selling ads on your blog is the most common form of revenue generation for bloggers. And there are many ways to do it that don't turn off your readers or interrupt your content. Ads, when used properly, can be a great way to make money on your blog without a whole lot of effort on your part. A popular way to get started is to sign up with an ad serving network, such as Google Adsense or Media.net. These networks will allow you to add a bit of code to your site, and they'll handle the rest, paying you for clicks that those ads generate. This is popular among bloggers because it requires very little effort. They have the advertisers already, and they handle every aspect of the process.

But for larger blogs, it may be worthwhile to sell the ads yourself.

By selling the ad space directly, you can make more money and ensure a certain amount of money per impression, or per month, without worrying just how many people click on the ad itself. Doing this may require you to go out and contact advertisers to get them interested, which takes more time and energy on your part. But this effort can pay off. And by including an advertiser information page on your site, you may get people contacting you instead of your having to go out and find them.

There are a number of other ways to put ads on your site that are less popular, but still very effective. Services like BlogAds.com will let you sign up, choose your own prices, and let advertisers contact you directly. Or Kontera.com will allow you to place ads in the form of text links within your posts, so you don't have to crowd your site with banners.

The key with advertising, as with most other forms of monetization mentioned here, is that the more readers you have, the more money you can make. For advertising especially, the money you can earn is directly tied to the traffic you have. Advertisers will be willing to pay a premium to reach a large audience.

This section on monetization is a great start, but there are many, many more ways that people are making money online. This was meant to provide you with a basic introduction to the ways bloggers make money.

Hopefully your creative juices are flowing. If you want more details on any of the ideas mentioned, or specific instructions on how to set them up, you can easily research them online. And they're all areas taught in much greater depth in the home-study "Professional Blogging" course taught by the New York Institute of Career Development (*nyicd.com*).

WHAT COMES NEXT

The blogosphere is big, and it's getting bigger. Hopefully this book has given you a greater sense of how the most successful bloggers among us are using the tools at their disposal to grow and earn money. But the dirty little secret of blogging, and the online space in general, is that it's constantly changing. The tips and advice provided in this book are a launching pad. While the fundamentals of branding provided here will never go out of style, the tools and techniques may change over time. Change happens fast in the digital age, and every successful blogger has a responsibility to stay up to date on what's going on in the blogosphere. Already today there are a couple of shifts taking place that are worth noting.

The first is the increased use of more *dynamic content*. We made note of this earlier in the book, but it's crucial to realize that bloggers now are providing more and more audio and video content in addition to plain text in order to attract new readers and keep old readers coming back for more.

Internet users have proven that their attention spans are getting shorter and shorter.

Whereas a traditional newspaper reader might be more than willing to sit down and read a two-page article, your blog's readers most likely won't. They want content they can consume in a hurry. They've come to expect to be quickly entertained.

When building a successful blog, you should account for this shift. Start experimenting with video content early on, and your likelihood of success will only go up.

The second shift is a change in the way we consume online content. Of course you'll want to include an RSS feed option for people who use an RSS reader. But that might not be enough anymore. Allowing people to subscribe via email or getting your content on social networks is vital to meeting your readers' needs. The motto here is "Be where your readers are."

More and more, people are browsing and consuming online content from phones and tablets.

This "mobile shift" is one you should pay close attention to. Already, companies large and small are becoming aware of the need to have a website that's optimized for mobile traffic. This means ensuring that people who visit your page from their phones can get the full experience.

If you use a Smartphone to browse the Web, you know how frustrating it can be when you visit a site that's practically unusable. The text is too small, the links are too close together, and you can't zoom. Most of the popular blogging platforms are already accounting for this device switch, but you should be aware of how your site looks on a phone or tablet, because that's how many people will end up coming to your blog.

The rest is up to you. Keep this book as a reference, but actively use it! The worst possible action for bloggers is to take no action at all. There's always something to be done to improve and build upon your brand. Hopefully this book has given you some ideas that you can put into practice. Hopefully it's opened your eyes to some new ways you can help grow your audience.

Now you know that you're a brand, and that everything you do online is an effort to build a successful blog that ties into that brand. A successful blog takes a lot of work. But the truth is, it's work that you're going to love.

Go forth and conquer!

RESOURCES AND FURTHER READING

AFFILIATE MARKETING PROGRAMS

Affiliate-program.amazon.com
Cj.com
Clickbank.com
Shareasale.com

ALERTS & ANALYTICS TOOLS

Alerts.yahoo.com
Bing.com/toolbox/webmaster
Google.com/alerts
Google.com/analytics
Web.analytics.yahoo.com

ARTICLE SUBMISSION WEBSITES

Ehow.com
Examiner.com
Ezinearticles.com
Hubpages.com
Squidoo.com

BLOGGING PLATFORMS

Blogger.com
Compendium.com
Movabletype.com
Squarespace.com
Tumblr.com
Typepad.com
Wordpress.com
Weebly.com

BLOGS ON BLOGGING

Blogherald.com
Copyblogger.com
Dailyblogtips.com
Doshdosh.com
Johnchow.com
Lorelle.wordpress.com
Performancing.com
Problogger.net
Quickonlinetips.com
Weblogtoolscollection.com

BLOGS ON BRANDING AND MARKETING

Acleareye.com
Brandmediaweek.typepad.com
Brandmix.blogspot.com
Ducttapemarketing.com
Socialmediaexplorer.com
Thebrandelelastic.com
Tomfishburne.com
Wheresthesausage.typepad.com
Zachhellermarketing.com

BOOKS ON BLOGGING

Blogging All in One for Dummies
by Susan M. Gunelius

*Blogging Tips: Confessions of a
Six Figure Blogger*
by Zac Johnson

*ProBlogger: Secrets for Blogging
Your Way to a Six-Figure Income*
by Darren Rowse

Social Networking for Career Success
by Miriam Salpeter

*The Secret to Writing a Successful
and Outstanding Blog*
by Liz Strauss

*101 Blogging Tips: How to Create a Blog That
People Will Find, Read, and Share*
by Tristan Higbee

BOOKS ON BRANDING

*Brand Against the Machine: How to Build Your
Brand, Cut Through the Marketing Noise, and Stand
Out from the Competition* by John Morgan

*Branding Yourself: How to Use Social Media to
Invent or Reinvent Yourself (2nd Edition)*
101 Branding Tips
by Ed Roach and Kim Hutchinson

BOOKS ON SEO

Search Engine Optimization for Dummies
by Peter Kent

The Truth About Search Engine Optimization
by Rebecca Lieb

The Art of SEO
by Eric Enge, Stephan Spencer,
Jessie Stricchiola and Rand Fishkin

DOMAIN NAME GENERATORS

Bustaname.com
Domainbots.com
Dotomator.com
Geek.name
Moniker.com/domainname.jsp
Namestation.com

DOMAIN NAME MARKETPLACES

Domainmarketplace.com
Domaintools.com
Dynadot.com/marketplace/about.html
Flippa.com
Sedo.com

DOMAIN REGISTRATION DATABASES

Archive.org/web/web.php
Networksolutions.com/whois/index.jsp

DOMAIN NAME REGISTRARS

Gandi.net
Godaddy.com
Name.com
Namecheap.com
Networksolutions.com
1and1.com
Register.com

E-BOOK SERVICES

Ebookit.com
EbookTemplate-Source.com
Scribd.com
Smashwords.com

FONT DISTRIBUTORS

Fontbureau.com
Fontshop.com
Fontspace.com
Myfonts.com
Vllg.com/fonts

KEYWORD RESEARCH TOOLS

Adwords.google.com
Analyticsdigger.org
Keyworddiscovery.com
Wordtracker.com
Wordze.com
Social media platforms
Facebook.com
Linkedin.com
Pinterest.com
Plus.google.com
Youtube.com
Twitter.com

WEB FEED MANAGEMENT PROVIDERS

Feedburner.google.com
Feedcat.net
Feed.informer.com
Mailchimp.com
Revresponse.com
Site.pheedo.com

WEBINAR SERVICES

MegaMeeting.com
Vyew.com
Webex.com
Yugma.com
Yuuguu.com

WEBSITES & BLOGS BY CONTRIBUTORS

Bigbrandsystem.com
Movablemedia.com
Roomfu.com/blog
Rosalindgardner.com
Successful-blog.com
Webislove.com
Zacjohnson.com
Design2Share.com

INDEX

Visit us at *nyicd.com/branding-for-bloggers*

Share your blogging stories with us, read more expert advice, and join our blogroll.

Books from Allworth Press

Allworth Press is an imprint of Skyhorse Publishing, Inc. Selected titles are listed below.

Starting Your Career as a Professional Blogger
by Jacqueline Bodnar (6 x 9, 192 pages, paperback, $19.95)

Starting Your Career as a Freelance Writer, Second Edition
by Moira Anderson Allen (6 x 9, 304 pages, paperback, $24.95)

Starting Your Career as a Freelance Web Designer
by Neil Tortorella (6 x 9, 256 pages, paperback, $19.95)

Starting Your Career as a Freelance Editor: A Guide to Working with Authors, Books, Newsletters, Magazines, Websites, and More
by Mary Embree (6 x 9, 240 pages, paperback, $19.95)

The Art of Digital Branding, Revised Edition
by Ian Cocoran (6 x 9, 272 pages, paperback, $19.95)

Emotional Branding: The New Paradigm for Connecting Brands to People, Updated and Revised Edition
by Marc Gobe (6 x 9, 352 pages, 134 b&w illustrations, paperback, $19.95)

Brand Thinking and Other Noble Pursuits
by Debbie Millman (6 x 9, 256 pages, hardcover, $29.95)

Branding for Nonprofits: Developing Identity with Integrity
by DK Holland (6 x 9, 208 pages, paperback, $19.95)

Brand Jam: Humanizing Brands Through Emotional Design
by Marc Gobé (6 x 9, 240 pages, paperback, $24.95)

The Pocket Small Business Owner's Guide to Starting Your Business on a Shoestring
by Carol Tice (5 ¼ x 8 ¼ , 224 pages, paperback, $14.95)

The Writer's Legal Guide
by Kay Murray and Tad Crawford (6 x 9, 352 pages, paperback, $19.95)

The Pocket Legal Companion to Copyright: A User-Friendly Handbook for Protecting and Profiting from Copyrights
by Lee Wilson (5 x 7 ½, 320 pages, paperback, $16.95)

The Pocket Legal Companion to Trademark: A User-Friendly Handbook on Avoiding Lawsuits and Protecting Your Trademarks
by Lee Wilson (5 x 7 ½, 320 pages, paperback, $16.95)

To see our complete catalog or to order online, please visit *www.allworth.com.*